# TRANSFORM YOUR BRAIN

## ONE THOUGHT AT AT TIME

*Stress Patterns, Anxiety and Overthinking Rewired*
*Second Edition*

**DOREEN STEENLAND**

Copyright © 2023 by Doreen Steenland,
Doreen Steenland Coaching & Facilitation, LLC

Second Edition © 2025 Doreen Steenland

ISBN: (digital) 979-8-9887404-0-7
ISBN: (paperback) 979-8-9887404-3-8

All rights reserved. No portion of the eBook, Paperback or Hardcover may be reproduced, stored in a retrieval system, or transmitted in any form or by any means—electronic, mechanical, photocopy, recording, scanning, or other, except for brief quotations in critical reviews or articles—without prior written permission of the copyright owner.

All Scripture quotations, unless otherwise indicated, are taken from the Holy Bible, New International Version®, NIV®. Copyright ©1973, 1978, 1984, 2011 by Biblica, Inc.™ Used by permission of Zondervan. All rights reserved worldwide. www.zondervan.com. The "NIV" and "New International Version" are trademarks registered in the United States Patent and Trademark Office by Biblica, Inc.™

Although I am a nurse by profession, all content and information in the book is for educational and informational purposes only and does not constitute medical advice, nor does it establish any kind of patient–client relationship. This information is not to be substituted for professional medical or mental health advice, and you should never rely solely on the information in this book for your health needs. Always consult a professional prior to making any professional, legal, medical, or financial decisions.

"The first act of love is the giving of attention"

---

**DALLAS WILLARD**

# Praise for Transform Your Brain, One Thought At At Time

"Transform Your Brain, One Thought At A Time" by Doreen Steenland is a treasure trove. Each compelling page contains captivating stories, fascinating insights and hard-earned wisdom gleaned from years of experience. I thoroughly enjoyed reading Doreen's fantastic book because the science is clear and the brain research accessible.

The icing on the cake are the bonus sections carefully placed throughout the book so we can reflect, digest and apply all the richness we are learning. This resource is not simply ingesting information. It is applying and practicing what we learn so we become our best selves to live abundantly and gracefully."

**Chris Coursey, Author of The Joy Switch and President of THRIVEtoday**

Get ready to embark on a journey of self-discovery and growth! "Transform Your Brain" by Doreen Steenland is an incredibly inspiring read that touched my heart deeply. Through her powerful words, Doreen taught me how to look inward and tap into my own mind, heart, and soul. Her guidance on transforming the brain is invaluable for anyone seeking personal growth and transformation. I am so grateful to Doreen for sharing her insights with the world and teaching us all how to transform our brains."

**Judy Go Wong, Author, Award Winning Filmmaker and Actress**

Doreen Steenland has shared her story in an authentic beautiful fashion. It is true that we all go through trauma and it is wonderful that her book adds another vehicle of knowledge for all of us to reflect upon and use to heal. The book is exceptionally well written and invites us to be curious as we join the author in exploring pathways to overcome trauma and live as our true authentic selves.

**M. Teresa Lawrence, Founder and Executive Director of the Trueness Project**

"Coach Doreen's book, *Transform Your Brain One Thought at a Time,* is a game-changer. I first read it on Kindle and ended up making 231 highlights. That alone tells you how rich it is! I later bought the hard copy so I could work through it again—more slowly and thoroughly.

What makes this book powerful is the way Doreen weaves together neuroscience, solid psychology, and biblical truth. She exposes the subconscious "operating systems" we inherit from our families or simply accept as "just the way we are." Then she shows us how real transformation is possible—helping us replace toxic reactions with healthy, life-giving responses.

Her insights guide us to rewire how we listen, think, feel, and act—leading to lasting patterns of growth and fruitfulness.

I highly recommend this book to anyone who wants to break free from old cycles and step into healthier ways of living—for themselves, their families, and their future."

**Tom Griffith, Urban Pastor for 34 years and Founder of Greater Formation**

**So Practical and Relatable**. Our brains are so powerful! I really resonated with how the book gave relatable information on using practical strategies to change our brain. Doreen shared personal stories that helped me to feel like she understood what my needs were. She also had a way of delving a little deeper in a way that felt very applicable and memorable. I will definitely use the strategies shared and use this book as a reference to go back to.

Rebekah Keizer
**Insightful content making brain science applicable**

"Transform Your Brain" is a captivating read that grabbed my attention from the very beginning. Doreen skillfully weaves valuable and technical information on brain science, effortlessly connecting it to relatable situations like driving, navigating heavy traffic, and reading maps—experiences we all share. Her ability to make complex concepts accessible speaks to her nursing and coaching background, adding a layer of credibility to the book.

What sets this book apart is the insightful content and the anticipation it builds. Putting it down is a challenge, and I can't wait to dive into the full-text cover-to-cover. Doreen's knack for making brain science understandable for the average person is truly commendable.

A delightful surprise at the end is the 5-page list of recommended reading. It's a treasure trove for those eager to explore further into the fascinating world of brain science. "Transform Your Brain" is not just a book; it's a journey that promises both enlightenment and practical insights—highly recommended!

**Laura C Sanders, Author of Your Daily Companion To The Bible**

Transform Your Brain is a blessing! Doreen has woven together much goodness from so many of the key thought leaders in the "brain space" and infused every page with her heart ... you will indeed transform as you enjoy soaking up the truths on each page!

**Scott Frickenstein**, PhD, Founder, Leading by Design

**One of Those Books You Gotta Read EVERY SINGLE Year!**

If I had to sum this book up in one phrase, it would be: "Emotional Liberation in Action"! I read lots of books and this is one of the most life-changing books I've ever read. My main reason for wanting to read this book was to discover how to quickly bounce back to a better frame of mind when I hit negative emotional and mental states.

That's extremely important to have because life will always happen. In this book, she taught me how to recognize and reroute the patterns that keep so many people stuck. This is very empowering because it's helped me unlock yet another layer of healing and growth!

The author has a big brain AND a big heart! She's gone through her own journey and has not only experienced these things anecdotally. She has the science behind how all of it works. Along with that, she demonstrates a strong sense of ethics and respectfully, and with humility, shows she's an expert on the subject.

Although this book contains lots of research and facts based in neurobiology, it felt like I was sitting right across the table, getting a glimpse inside of the author's heart and mind. Doreen knows how to take what would normally be some pretty heavy stuff to digest, and place it into a very practical and fun to engage with.

The best books aren't the ones that just have a bunch of information, the best books are the ones that actually make you think or behave differently. If you or someone you know wants to learn how to gain more control over your mind and emotions, this book is an absolute game-changer! You gotta get it and read it not just once, but multiple times!

**Dak Frederick Writing Coach And Author**

Don't let stress short circuit your ability to love! Neuro-informed nurse Doreen Steenland gives a master class on how to live life to the fullest with love and consideration for others. It is thoroughly researched and filled with compelling narrative. Though it is written from the perspective of a Christian, it is geared toward a broader audience. Anyone can benefit from this awesome book.

**Paul M. Burns,**
**Author of Becoming Spiritually Intelligent**

"This book is something I have long looked for! It contains the map and the process that I have been on but gives definitive and descriptive words to help me navigate the next level of healing I am on personally. Living with trauma, battling it so many times, knowing it exists and navigating it "to the best of my ability and God's help" has long been my life statement. I have sought wise counsel, healing prayer, and deliverance from my Deliverer Himself. This book assists in this process, giving succinct, clear tools to use that will help heal many. Thank you, Doreen, for listening to the Lord to bring this valuable resource to the desperately broken world. I am grateful for your obedience and the efforts you have put forth into summarizing your journey and then sharing it with us all."

**Pamela Mertz,
Author and Founder of Blueprint Life**

From the first chapter, I was hooked! I could see myself in the pages.

I feel empowered that with the tools provided in "transform your mind" I can identify my stress patterns and live full with peace, joy and confidence!

**Andie Plunkett**

"There just are no words to describe how impactful this is! From the foreword defining who God is and redefining the word "Christianity" to the end, I was filled with so many "nuggets" that when I saw the synopsis at the end of each chapter I literally was like YESSSS!!!!!! I loved it.

**Deborah Marini, MA,
Founder of The Awareness Impact**

# TABLE OF CONTENTS

Introduction: Withness as a Witness Of Love ........................................ 1

Chapter 1: A Professional Eggshell Walker ........................................... 5

Chapter 2: The Space Between the Journey and Your Destination .... 17

Chapter 3: What in the World (Brain) Is Going On? ............................ 22

Chapter 4: The Two Main Regions of the Brain ................................... 31

Chapter 5: Holy Noticing: Attention to the Right Things ................... 43

Chapter 6: On the Road ......................................................................... 52

Chapter 7: Changing Your Route on the Fly ....................................... 61

Chapter 8: Lane Closures Ahead
(The Express Highway to Possibility) ................................................... 75

Chapter 9: The Saboteurs Working Behind the Scenes ...................... 86

Chapter 10: Change the Channel .......................................................... 94

Chapter 11: The Express Highway to Possibility .............................. 101

Chapter 12: Emotional Attunement .................................................... 118

Chapter 13: The Perfect Flow of Traffic ............................................. 122

Chapter 14: Mindfulness, Mindsight, and Mutual Mind .................. 127

Chapter 15: Danger AHEAD ................................................................ 136

Chapter 16: From Emotional Slavery to Emotional Liberation ........ 144

Chapter 17: Trauma .............................................................................. 156

Chapter 18: Quiet Quitting/ Quiet Cracking ..................................... 174

Chapter 19: Medical Professionals .................................................................. 179

Chapter 20: On Burnout ............................................................................ 189

Chapter 21: The Power of Presence: Leading From a Place of
Authenticity ............................................................................................ 203

Chapter 22: Parents of Teenagers .................................................................. 208

Chapter 23: Wave Watchers: Listening and Observing
the Waves ............................................................................................... 227

Chapter 24: Deep Waters .............................................................................. 240

Chapter 25: Decision Fatigue and the Brain ...................................................... 258

Glossary .................................................................................................. 263

References .............................................................................................. 280

Acknowledgments ................................................................................... 291

INTRODUCTION

# WITHNESS AS A WITNESS OF LOVE

---◆---

This book is not a religious treatise, nor is it a thesis on interpersonal neurobiology, positive intelligence, somatic coaching, or any of the other disciplines discussed here. The intent is not evangelical. I will not ask you to believe what I believe, for that is your choice. Those who have taught me and have gone before me through their research have shaped this book. My teachers have been many, as are the lessons you will encounter. The purpose of this work is for us to see each other compassionately in our humanity, connect with each other, and positively affect one another.

What I would like you to consider is that this book explores what occurs internally when we are daily triggered into reactions instead of intentional responses.

This book is about us individually and collectively as a society as we interact with creation and the Creator.

I realize that the word Christian holds negative connotations for some who have been adversely affected by the church or professing believers. This is bound to happen when someone's words and actions don't match; however, this is the human condition. I ask forgiveness for the Christians in this world who have misrepresented the God of the universe, of which, I have also been guilty. If you proclaim belief in the God of the universe, your love should be a witness to His perfect love. I know full well I have not always shown that love, as you will see in this book, and I ask for grace as I show up perfectly imperfect in this bold assignment.

I believe that there is one Creator of the universe. God is love, and the Bible says He sent Immanuel, God with us, to be connected and in relationship with us personally. I realize the reader may not hold similar viewpoints. I would ask you to consider your source of strength, love, and energy as you read the word "God" throughout this book. The Withness Nuggets may be a source of internal conflict for you. What I ask is that as you read, you get curious about the trigger and practice remaining relational. This is the work for us collectively, as human beings.

I see this book as an intentional gym to practice self-regulation and co-regulation when your brain feels dysregulated or when you feel resistance. This is personal for me. As an overcomer of trauma and a highly successful, over-committed professional, I came to realize that many of the tactics that drove my success were draining me dry. They were exhausting my mind, body, and spirit — they were no longer serving me. These patterns were now hurting me and holding me back from living a peaceful life.

I believe that self-regulation and co-regulation are missing ingredients for living present and lovingly in a disconnected world. Those who have mastered this have developed the ability to create psychological safety for those who differ from them. Amy Edmondson describes psychological safety in her book "The Fearless Organization." We need psychological safety to thrive in a world full of threats and uncertainty. As a result of her research, she coined the term "psychological safety," which means (and I paraphrase) the ability to be seen, heard, and understood without interpersonal fear holding you back or hindering your performance.

Psychological safety is more about an atmosphere of vulnerability; risk taking; hearing all the voices to tap into the collective wisdom of the group, not just the loudest; and problem-solving from the relational circuitry in one's brain. It's not about avoiding problems or faking positivity. Only when we acknowledge and embrace our differences can we explore solutions for the world's problems. It is my passion to equip others to be psychologically safe people who grow authentically, without fear of judgment or repercussion, and who give space for others to do likewise.

As I say this, I know fully that we were created for belonging. Your brain is wired to connect deeply with those who are "like you." As humans, we look at the outward appearances to determine this likeness, but God looks at the heart (1 Samuel 16:7). Psychological safety is about respecting, challenging, and collaborating through our relational circuitry instead of reacting in competition or scarcity because our brain has gone offline. It is about reducing threats and maximizing rewards in our brain, as well as the intention and regulation of one's inner being. It is about humbling ourselves as we look with eyes of love instead of shame, blame, and condemnation, which come from the fear circuitry in the brain. We will look at the scientifically proven "triggers" that cause internal reactions, diminish psychological safety, and amplify threats.

This book is about BEING love and healing the world as we connect with ourselves, others, and God authentically. Throughout this book you will see the analogy of a map and roadways. Note that this is not a perfect word picture of your brain's neural pathways, but I believe you will follow the train of thought — please patiently work with me.

Remember, if you do not agree with the Christian worldview, this will be an exercise of curiosity and self-regulation for you. Practicing in this space will give you the tools you need to tackle the daily tension one experiences internally when with those who think differently. If you hold a Christian worldview, the things that you hear in this book may seem foreign; I encourage you to maintain the same curiosity and allow yourself to be open-minded and stretch your relationship with God to new levels of depth.

If you are ready to enter the gym and learn new tools of self- and co-regulation, then this book is for you. Join me on this journey of intimacy with self, others, and God by applying the proven scientific disciplines described here. For those whose curiosity becomes sparked about the God in whom I believe, please reach out to me personally for a conversation.

CHAPTER 1

# A PROFESSIONAL EGGSHELL WALKER

◆

The house smelled of pot roast. My young brain quickly searched my subconscious and connected my memories. The simmering beef with bay leaves was a distinct, welcoming smell. Walking into the kitchen, the light was shining through the sliding glass doors, and I immediately felt hot — but it wasn't from the light shining in. The room actually had a darkness about it. My face flushed, and there was a burning sensation that traveled from my stomach to the top of my head. A low-level hum of anxiety filled the space in my chest as my breathing became shallow. I braced myself for a tsunami.

The look on his face spelled trouble, and the silence was deadly. He stood with his arms crossed and a stiff body. The absence of a smile clarified that some sort of conflict had occurred prior to my arrival, and it was creating tension. My senses immediately went on three-alarm-fire alert; I could see below the surface to what was actually happening. My insides churned and burned with discomfort, as this was now my problem. No filter could protect me from the assault on my nervous system. Besides the runaway visceral reaction, waves of emotions pounded relentlessly, crashing in on me and carrying me out to a sea of turmoil where I had no choice or control.

To keep from drowning in the churning waves, I instinctively became a professional eggshell walker. I tiptoed around to keep an internal state of calm. It was a subconscious technique that sometimes brought calm, but it never worked for long.

This walking-on-eggshells pattern was a well-worn pathway in my brain. When this pattern didn't work, I had others to fall back on. Cue the overachieving pattern. Maybe if I did enough or performed well enough, then surely there would be internal peace.

In reality, peace was always an illusion — no matter what I did, it was never enough. I was never enough!

I subconsciously trained myself to believe that these stress patterns — automatic pathways that had developed to help me deal with stress — were helpful for me, when in fact they actually increased my internal pain. Years later, I had grown and matured into a successful and accomplished woman — on the outside; on the inside, I was still living life on high alert. The high-functioning human people saw when they looked at me was only that way because I went to great lengths (subconsciously using my stress patterns) to hide the turmoil in which I was living.

These two patterns traveled with me from childhood to adulthood and affected every aspect of my life and all my relationships. For years, the questions "Why are you so sensitive?" and "Why are you so emotional?" haunted me, as if I were a defective product with a no-return policy. For years I thought I was alone, only to find out that residual trauma is a common plight.

I had had enough. But I will pause my story … for now.

Millions of people struggle because they default to stress patterns as their primary way of dealing with stress. One stress pattern might work in the beginning, but most people will adapt and try others throughout his/her lifetime. This is because stress patterns are not the proper solution to the problem. But most people aren't consciously aware of the dysfunction going on in their lives; if they are, they are at a complete loss how to deal with it. As a result, people adopt a new stress pattern to deal with their problems.

These patterns are a quick fix for the deeper excavation that needs to happen in a person's internal landscape. My brain had been training for this my whole life, and so has yours.

Stress is a natural part of life, and we have no choice but to deal with it. There are different types and levels of stress too, from annoying, day-to-day inconveniences to major life events. The question is, how do you deal with stressors? We can choose to respond thoughtfully and with intentionality, OR we will subconsciously react out of our emotions. Either way, the resulting manner of dealing with stress dictates a person's thoughts and actions.

Before we get the wrong idea and paint stress as bad, I'd like you to consider that some stress is necessary and good for you. Stress serves its purposes and affects the whole human body.

It is often a motivator that propels us into action, but chronic stress is toxic for your body, mind, and spirit and leads to premature aging, disease, pain syndromes, and whole-body inflammation.

Stress patterns, for this book, are the go-to behaviors, thoughts, and emotions — most times subconscious — that we default to when we face chronic stress or cognitive overload. Stress patterns are maladaptive defense mechanisms we use to manage the discomfort of stress. Many live a lifetime without even noticing how these stress patterns are affecting their happiness and their relationships — but you are different, because you are here.

The good news is that we can rewire maladaptive stress patterns and build positive coping mechanisms — healthy ways of dealing with stress. Your emotions will often serve as data points for us. Emotions are neither good nor bad; they are just information that we get to process. They are mile markers on the road to wellness. This is the work we will be doing.

Regardless of the type and level of stress, the human brain's No. 1 function is ensuring safety. It does this with coping mechanisms or stress patterns. As stress patterns (like the ones mentioned above) become more ingrained, they control a person's life to the point he/she no longer behaves like his/her true self. The person sacrifices his/her authentic self to fulfill his/her basic human needs (Maslow's hierarchy of needs).

For me, as a registered nurse and certified professional coach through the International Coaching Federation (the equivalent of the American Medical Association in medicine), science-based approaches to solving my ineffective stress patterns were mandatory as I reflected on my life's stories.

There were things I knew instinctively that needed to be validated by science. I was also keenly aware that my brain will always find what it is looking for — so will yours. The brain loves to prove itself right — it's called "confirmation bias" — as well as keep you safe – that's its job. I needed scientific data, and recent functional MRI (fMRI)-centered research and factor analysis research provided the needed evidence.

Thankfully, neuroscientists, interpersonal neurobiologists, doctors, and top thought leaders in modern psychology have tirelessly given their lives to advance what we know about the brain and have written about these concepts extensively.

So I dove in the deep end. I pursued multiple certifications in the neuroscience of change, considering the whole person — body, mind, and spirit. I realized what happened in my mind had also grown like a cancer in my body. My muscle tension and other physical symptoms were anecdotal evidence that led me to seek a holistic approach to the science.

My resume includes hundreds of hours of study in and application of neuroscience-of-change training, trauma-informed training, and somatic training, as well as devouring hundreds of books by those who have devoted their lives to these types of work. But as a believer in a creative, brilliant, and indescribable God, it was important to me I did not leave God behind in this scientific exploration to wellness, especially since this book was His idea planted in my heart.

I think it's important you understand why I specifically included trauma-informed training in my studies. First, statistics show 50% of all people have experienced trauma. That's half of the world's population, which is a pretty big deal to me. And since fMRI data has proven that those who have experienced trauma have a narrow "window of tolerance"* it's an important concept that we will explore throughout this book.

Second, based on my work with client after client and research I have studied, it is apparent that unresolved trauma is a plague in the United States. Many people have undergone years of therapy and have healed significantly. They are high-functioning, successful humans who contribute to the world in big ways; however, residual effects from a narrow window of tolerance and maladaptive stress patterns remain (Siegel, 2020b).

Third, trauma recovery has been personal for me. I am proof that you can return to a joyful and peaceful life after traumatic events and live a next-level life; however, failing to address my trauma was a limiting factor for the first 30 years of my healing journey.

The final pressing reason for writing this book is more statistics. According to the latest statistics from The American Institute of Stress (n.d.), about 33% of people report feeling extreme stress, 77% of people experience stress that affects their physical health, and 48% of people have trouble sleeping because of stress, and Hull adds that 73% of people have stress that affects their mental health (2023).

"Houston, we have a [stress] problem!"[1]

To solve this problem, we need to travel to the inner world and pave new pathways in the brain. This includes learning new ways of responding to replace old stress patterns.

It has been a personal journey of discovery and an investment of time, money, and space — and it's been so worth it.

Don't worry if the stress patterns I've described so far are not the same as yours. There are eight other stress patterns that are common to our culture, and yours are as unique as the distractors you use to hide them. We will discover them throughout our journey together, as you apply these principles to your own life.

You will understand what is happening in your brain, because awareness is the first step toward change.

You will recognize the signs and symptoms of your stress patterns before they take over.

You will discover the forces behind your stress patterns, enabling you to change the dysfunctional patterns that are actually hindering your healing and growth.

It's possible to experience your emotions without stuffing them, numbing them, or brushing them off. Your emotions (as well as other stimuli) are energy that is both experienced and sent to

---

[1] *The window of tolerance [coined by Dr. Daniel Siegel] is the "optimal zone of [emotional and energetic] arousal" that allows you to respond to stress and the demands of daily life effectively. When in the window of tolerance, one bounces back quickly under stressful circumstances — fully able to manage one's emotions and think clearly from a space of harmony. When one leaves the window of tolerance they can become hyper-aroused or hypo-aroused.

your brain as data, which your brain reacts to. Ignoring the data is causing yourself physical pain and training yourself to live a compartmentalized life. We will learn to accept the data, process it, and move forward appropriately.

Imagine interpreting that energy and quickly returning to a balanced state of mind.

You can develop resilience — the ability to bounce back quickly — even in high-stress situations.

You will learn to tap into the circuitry of your brain that promotes love, connection, joy, confidence, calm, and clear, focused action, because you will hear from God and experience life to the full. Throughout this book, I will discuss "withness," which is a created word, not a typo. I use this word to describe one of the key elements of learning presence. At the end of each chapter, I will present "Withness Nuggets." Each nugget will invite you to partner with God in your healing journey and perhaps see your relationship with Him from a new perspective.

Imagine a deep connection with others and affecting them positively because you are living as your authentic self — seen, heard, understood, and known.

It's time to unmask and discover the real you! It's time to discern your best path to calm and confident authenticity. Through this decision, you will take steps to rewire the stress patterns that trip you up, so you can walk courageously and return to joy quickly when you become dysregulated.

You will be aware when your perception of your inner and outer worlds are off and quickly shift back to a place of true internal calm. You will have the tools to intercept the old pathways and strip them of their control, allowing you to choose new pathways and take back your power and your life!

Your joy, peace, and confidence will skyrocket and become contagious. Hang on, because we are about to go deep into your brain to discover the joy and peace you've been searching for.

For those who are looking for the footnote version of this journey, you can get it here.

 **FREE Resource Here**

Grab Your Free Resource Here:

Shrink Your Stress Playbook:
With Reset Rituals from the
Micro-Shift Reset System®

Science Backed Micro-Shifts
for real-time relief

https://DoreenSteenland.com/shrink-your-stress-playbook

## Withness Nugget:

We get to choose.

We get to choose life — not a cruise control life but an abundant life. Cruise control life is unconscious and unattached. Those living on cruise control react to stimuli and circumstances from survival strategies developed throughout their lifetime. In order to change this pattern of living, a shift of attention away from the things that no longer serve you toward the things that do is needed. "Where your attention goes, neural firing flows and neural connections grow"(Siegel,2019, p.17).

We hear from and connect with God from the relational circuitry of the brain. With this understanding, we move from rules and religion to a relationship with God. It empowers us to move the information from head knowledge to heart-centered wholeness with God from a space of being.

This is "withness as a witness," and we get to choose to attach intentionally to God, others, and ourselves from our body, mind, and spirit, which is what Jesus meant when He said, "Love the Lord your God with all your heart and with all your soul and with all your mind and with all your strength. The second is this: 'Love your neighbor as yourself.' There is no commandment greater than these" Mark 12:30-31 (NIV). It is an invitation to engage with Him, in life, and in your present moment. This is what we will be about in our time together, tackling our survival responses and clinging to LIFE Himself. We will do this through transforming our minds, one thought at a time.

## Mindful Moments:

Take a moment and notice your breathing.

Notice the depth or shallowness of your breath. Notice the air moving in and out of your lungs and the temperature of the air as it enters and exits your nostrils. Now, take three slow, deep breaths: inhale for a count of four, and exhale for a count of six. If you get distracted, don't judge yourself. Gently just return to breathing.

- What did you notice about your breathing?
- What did you discover after your three deep breaths? In your body? In your mind?

 **Journal Your Reflections:**

Reflect on your body and record any new sensations you notice, putting descriptive words on paper. Where in your body do you notice this sensation? Is there tension or weightlessness? Temperature changes? Is there a feeling or numbness? Notice your patterns from a place of curiosity — no judgment allowed.

- What do you desire in your life?
- Where is your attention going?
- What shift needs to occur?
- What patterns are you noticing?

CHAPTER 2

# THE SPACE BETWEEN THE JOURNEY AND YOUR DESTINATION

———◆———

When I was a kid, I remember learning how to read a map. The purpose of this was to teach us how to get from point A to point B quickly and efficiently. Back then, these foldable paper maps were free from AAA prior to a road trip. We used the maps to plan the route to and to arrive safely at our destination.

It was always fascinating to see the twists, turns, intersections, bypasses, and all the ways the various connections could lead us to our destination.

There are roadways that run north to south and others that run east to west, each with multitudes of offramps leading to other roads and different places. Some roadways go through mountains, and others go around those mountains. Some go through tunnels under waterways, and others are bridges above the waterways. These roadways give us access and connection to anywhere in the country.

One specific road can travel through dozens of states, so when we ask where does the road start, it's often unclear.

The same is true in our brains!

Just like roadways on a map, there are many pathways that lead to the unique structures within our brain, with each structure having a very specific function. As brain science advances, we learn more about the pathways, the connections, and their locations in the brain. Thankfully, with modern day advancements of fMRI, we no longer need to guess; we can actually trace many of these pathways.

For our purposes, the specific structures in the brain and their functions aren't important; we're learning more and more every day, so specifics can actually change. What is important for us right now is the general functioning of our brains regarding how we deal with stress. We will discover the pathways that travel through two different regions — the one you travel through most (survive), and the one you've been through before but not for a long time (thrive) — and explore how these pathways and regions affect your relationships, your happiness, your actions, and your sense of connectedness with other human beings.

Sometimes you experience traffic, construction, or detours on the roadways. These can prevent us from getting to our destinations on time, which is frustrating when we become attached to a route that is comfortable for us. In order to arrive at our destination, we need to be flexible and willing to adjust our route. We can choose another route, and it may even improve your view during your travels. You are the driver, and you are responsible for how you operate your vehicle. You have a choice: You can sit in traffic, frustrated and angry, or you can choose an alternative route. It's all up to you as the driver. I don't know about you, but that thought alone is freeing for me. I am not a victim of my circumstances; I can choose to respond with intention. I get to step into my power as the vehicle operator and determine not only my route but also my destination.

When you encounter an unforeseen hindrance along your route, as the driver, you can choose your next move from two different places. One space is where you intentionally choose your route, your speed, and your lane changes. You can choose to pause and check out the scenery. During this pause, you get to examine what influencers are traveling with you — and challenge their necessity. This is what I call conscious living. The other option is cruise control. On cruise control, you're not fully present because you don't have to give your full attention to driving; you're driving subconsciously. We live most of our lives here. This kind of life is boring, disengaged, and disconnected. It leaves people feeling like their day-to-day existence is mundane. Now, sometimes cruise control is helpful and good, but not normally. When we become aware — conscious participants in our travels — we experience an abundance of sensations, thoughts, connections, and intimacy. This is the abundant life, and all you need to do is choose to be a participant in the experiences of life. The abundant life is a life lived in connection to your unique essence, where you function as you were created to function — in connection with yourself, others, and God.

Which route you take when traveling is up to you. There are routes that take you places you've never been before, where a map is invaluable; and places you've visited multiple times, where you know the routes so well a map is unnecessary. Your brain has pathways you rarely take through the most important — yet seldom visited — region of your brain, which is what I'd like to help you find.

# Transform Your Brain

### Withness Nugget:

God has designed your brain, your body, and your spirit to work together in an integrated way. Our stress patterns and cruise-control living keep us dysregulated. Integrating our body, mind, and spirit leads to experiencing harmony and authentic connection with God, self, and others, as well as all the fruit of the Spirit. When dysregulated, we experience chaos and rigidity in their many forms and manifestations.

The abundant life is an integrated life of connection and purpose. Your brain will always find what it's looking for. What are you training it to look for?

### Mindful Moments:

Today, notice any tension in your body. Bring your focus to that tension.
- What sensations do you notice?
- Is there a temperature difference?
- What stands out to you? Get curious.
- What might that tension be trying to communicate to you?

### Journal Your Reflections:

- Consider your most traveled pathways. This is an internal state of being. Which state is your go-to — harmony, or chaos and rigidity?
- Do not judge it or condemn yourself. Today is about noticing.
- What patterns are you noticing? Reflect on your body and record any new sensations you notice, putting descriptive words on paper. Where in your body do you notice this sensation? Is there tension or weightlessness? Temperature changes? Is there a feeling or numbness? Notice your patterns from a place of curiosity — no judgment allowed.

CHAPTER 3

# WHAT IN THE WORLD (BRAIN) IS GOING ON?

———◆———

All creatures in the animal kingdom are hard-wired with the ability to self-protect, including humans. What sets us apart from the rest of the animals is the human brain processes information and makes reasoned decisions that keep us safe from harm. Your nervous system communicates with your brain by converting internal and external stimuli into data the brain understands. Through that communication, your brain will either draw you toward or away from the stimuli's source, be it a circumstance, sensation, person, place, or thing. While your brain and body are communicating, they release neurochemicals that begin the firing of specific neural pathways — the roadways in the brain.

Besides looking to be right, the brain is also a predicting machine. It predicts what will harm you and what will keep you safe. Experiences that proved to be rewards or threats shape these predictions, forming our brain pathways and our resulting behaviors.

For example, in my opening story, when I walked into the kitchen and saw the look on his face and his body language, my brain was predicting danger because I'd seen both before. This began a neurochemical release and a subconscious reaction, which I experienced physically as heat. The brain and body worked together so that I'd recognize the threatening situation and react to keep myself safe. From there, my brain went to my go-to stress pattern that had kept me safe in the past — eggshell walking. If you reread that opening story, you can walk through how my body and brain were working together.

When a situation occurs, your brain identifies it as a reward or threat and files it away so it can predict what might happen if a similar situation or circumstance occurs. All of this happens subconsciously and automatically. By the time your brain adds thoughts to the initial stimuli, the body has already experienced the sensations that normally accompany those thoughts. And when we're in the survive region, we more often than not judge self, others, and circumstances negatively.

When threatened, the body sends all the blood (and therefore the oxygen it carries) to the large muscles in the legs and arms so that we can survive the danger (fight, flight, freeze/faint, or fawn reaction). This is the base animal reaction for self-protection and goes back to the days when we needed to protect ourselves from lions, tigers, bears, poisonous plants, and all the dangers of wilderness living. To increase blood supply to the large muscles, we must divert it from other places — and this includes the prefrontal cortex, which is where executive function occurs in the brain. This explains why we cannot think clearly when we're triggered or threatened. You might have heard of people saying things like, "I just froze and could not respond in the moment." This is survival mode. When we are acting from the subconscious protective mechanism, we are surviving the threat. This threat reaction was not created to be a long-term solution to threats — it was temporary. Sadly, with all the stimuli — both internal and external — that we are constantly processing, many of us have adopted survival mode as our go-to way of life. The effects consist of feeling overwhelmed, stressed, anxious, and unable to rest and digest. Fear, failure, and frustration rule the survive region, and it is the region your brain chooses on the regular. But you don't have to just survive — you can do so much more if you process threats and stress in the second region — the thrive region.

Don't think of the regions as specific locations. The neural pathways throughout your brain, like the roads on a map, are going every which way, connecting all sorts of structures, and the pathways are specific to each region. Taken together, the pathways of each region are the circuitry of that region. So there are specific survive pathways that comprise the survive circuitry, and the survive circuitry as a whole is the survive region. And the same is true with respect to the thrive pathways, circuitry, and region.

But before we look at these two regions in more depth, it's important to understand stress. Stress is something we sense — whether the source is internal or external — and we respond to this sense to protect ourselves from danger. This stress reaction is our nervous system telling us that a stimulus requires attention or action. This is a fact. And in our society, there are many things screaming for our attention.

It reminds me of the first time I visited New York City's Times Square during the holidays, where the energy is palpable. Your nervous system goes into overdrive. Thousands of people are hurrying through the streets, flowing like cattle at the control of a skilled rancher. The flow is fast and furious — until you get to an intersection. Paying attention to the streetlights and walk signs is important — if you value your life! One false move and you could step into an onslaught of moving, honking vehicles or fast-moving bicycles trying to beat the light.

You can always tell the newbies to the city by their reckless disregard to the flow of foot traffic. They stand out like a sore thumb, oblivious to city norms.

Who can blame the newbies — the stimuli is great! The lights are dazzling.

The poor and homeless and the ultra-wealthy line the same streets. Multiethnic skin colors, garments, languages, live music, and entertainment are all around you. The sensory stimuli entering from the outside world is real! It's possible, just from this description, you are feeling the energy that your brain is bringing to mind.

The overwhelm of stimuli is not just present in cities but in most environments, and it all affects our energy.

What about where you work? For instance, in a hospital, there are multitudes of sounds (alarms, machines, announcements), smells (antiseptics, various odors of illness, coffee in a break room), and movement (the hustle and bustle of staff, and patients and visitors wandering about).

What about technology? Your phone, the television, and the internet provide never-ending access to emails, texts, amber alerts, streaming reels, and talking heads with breaking news. Noise and information all the time, every day, regardless of where you are! The amount of external stimuli is overwhelming, yet it's "normal."

"We live in an attention economy. Human knowledge once doubled every thousand years; today, it's every 12 hours! No wonder we can't keep up" (Oberbrunner, n.d.). The fact remains: "Where your attention goes[,] your energy or legacy flows" (Oberbrunner, 2021). The constant stimuli from external sources affects your peace of mind.

Brain science can help us navigate the effects of these amplified technological advances, yet it seems the drive to keep up with all the stimuli leaves us feeling like we are living on a perpetually moving hamster wheel.

The Creator equipped our brains with filters to prevent the external stimuli from overwhelming us. These filters take the information coming in and pick a pathway to send the stimuli on — which is through one of the two regions of the brain — where a chain reaction begins.

As if all that external stimuli weren't overwhelming enough, we also have to deal with internal stimuli. The internal stimuli is your thoughts, feelings, beliefs, perspectives, values, standards, desires, biases (known and unknown), and expectations. And, as applicable, your brain attaches this internal stimuli to the incoming external stimuli.

Most of us recognize that these internal stimuli can create stress, and one form of internal stimuli is what we say to ourselves, such as the (often mean) inner critic talk that says all the things to yourself that you would never say to a friend.

And this is where we begin to understand how we can change our stress patterns into coping mechanisms.

These negative internal stimuli come from the survive region, where we judge, condemn, and place ourselves, others, and our circumstances on trial. This thinking and reacting is automatic according to the stress patterns that have developed. Disrupting these patterns is essential, as they cause broken relationships and discontent in the long run.

There are hundreds of tactics on managing external stimuli, and you can all probably list them in unison … cue the eye roll. This book tackles the internal reactions that keep us functioning on cruise control and living with regret. Regret comes when we repeatedly do the things we don't want to do.

Does this sound familiar? You wake up and start your day with great intention, only to have your plans foiled (again) by midafternoon. If you're hungry, angry, lonely, tired, or overwhelmed, the internal stimuli becomes even more difficult to manage. Your capacity diminishes and your brain goes into cruise-control mode, sending you on the path of least resistance. This is where your stress patterns come into play. You try to white-knuckle it through, only to be discouraged again.

And this discouragement amplifies the volume of the inner voices that criticize, condemn, and judge. As these voices grow in volume, your brain looks for evidence to support these "facts." As I mentioned before, your brain is always looking for confirmation of what it's telling itself. It's just doing its job and knows no better. If this is at all familiar, notice this today.

The thrive region is where we want to operate. The pathways of the thrive region move us toward relationship with others. We were created to connect and affect, and it's from the thrive region we can discern the next best steps to do so. The thrive pathways comprise the relational circuitry, accessing the executive functioning in the brain. Here, there are intentionality and responsiveness — the space of powerful decision-making. The thrive pathways enable us to connect with ourselves (identity), others (empathy and compassion), and God (wisdom and love), and look at our circumstances as possibilities, opportunities, and gifts. When we are functioning from the thrive region, we experience love, joy, and peace. When we are functioning from this region, we are in a harmonious state — in the window of tolerance. We will discuss the window of tolerance later, but for our purposes now, it is the optimal zone of arousal and influence. The sensory pathways are quick on-ramps to this highway, sort of like a fast pass to the thrive region of your brain.

The brain's circuitry runs through various structures of the brain to link them with other structures. When we choose the thrive circuitry, we can respond to challenges with our coping mechanisms. These coping mechanisms help us remain balanced and inside the window of tolerance. When our brain subconsciously runs the show through the survive circuitry, we react from our maladaptive defense mechanisms — our stress patterns.

Stress patterns are learned subconscious habits that we automatically turn to when we become dysregulated and leave the window of tolerance. Many times, stress patterns have helped us survive threats and trauma; but like I said before, they are not long-term solutions. I'd like to leave you with hope. Disrupting stress patterns allows thoughts to be redirected in your brain toward thrive pathways. You can intentionally take the exit ramp to the thrive highway instead of staying stuck on the survive highway.

### Withness Nugget:

God did not intend for you to go through life alone. Immanuel, which means "God is with us," desires for you to shift your gaze and choose Him. Where you place your attention will determine your spiritual and emotional maturity. Today, notice your go-to patterns when you're triggered. Where in your body do you experience the sensation? When you experience that sensation, what do you do to stop experiencing it? Where do you turn?

Do you judge yourself, others, and God harshly? If so, just know that God does not reside in this region of the brain. The Spirit that flows from our connection to Him is unconditional love. Judgment and love do not flow within the same circuitry in the brain.

Jim Wilder reminds us of this quote by Saint Claire of Assisi (1194–1253), who said: "We become what we love[,] and who we love shapes what we become." Wilder goes on to say, "Neuroscience would add that the beloved one becomes our life, our desire, and the one who sees us as we truly are. ... Are we so poorly attached to God that we cannot see or share His character?" (Renovated, 2020, pg.74–75).

God is love, and those who love Him will love others (1 John 4:16). When you notice your stressors, your brain chooses love or judgment and fear. These are the two distinct types of pathways in your brain that can be taken, and they are processed in different brain regions.

Just a note: Judgment and discernment are not the same. Many wrap judgment in the godly cloak of discernment. Notice this today for yourself if this comes up.

### Mindful Moments:

Close your eyes (if it feels comfortable to you) and listen to the sounds all around you. Now see if you can place your focus on the sound that is furthest away, bringing all your attention to that sound. Now shift your focus to the sound that is closest to you. Take a few deep breaths. What did you discover with this exercise?

### Journal Your Reflections:

- As you notice your internal and external stressors, what is coming up for you?
- Where in your body can you notice the effects of stress? Just notice — don't judge.
- What intentional shift can you make today?
- What patterns are you noticing? Reflect on your body and record any new sensations you notice, putting descriptive words on paper. Where in your body do you notice this sensation? Is there tension or weightlessness?

CHAPTER 4

# THE TWO MAIN REGIONS OF THE BRAIN

―――◆―――

Imagine being on a road trip. You're following your planned route, when suddenly you are on a four-lane highway of bumper-to-bumper traffic. Your GPS is telling you to get off on the next exit, but you are in the far left lane and trapped by semis, with no way to change lanes. Before you know it, you've missed your exit and there isn't another one for hundreds of miles, and there's also no way to turn around — there's an enormous construction wall dividing the highway. The traffic pattern is in charge — you have no control!

The flow of traffic forced you in a direction you did not want to travel. Suddenly, you feel anxiety bubbling to the surface. You beat yourself up! Your inner critic berates you for your predicament. The brain looks for a way to take back control of the situation. Your vision is dim, and everything seems hopeless. The circumstances have you in victim mode. Life is happening to you and not as you had planned.

All you can think about is escaping the current route and surviving this nightmare. Your brain takes you to your normal way of reacting to life's challenges. You may be furious, you may withdraw, or you may check out. If you have passengers in the car with you, you may get snappy and short with them.

At this very moment, you are traveling a familiar neural pathway that is tried and true. Your breathing is shallow and you keep condemning yourself for being so stupid to miss the turn. Maybe you choose to blame other drivers for not letting you over or your passengers for not telling you about the exit.

Everything appears bleak. Then you notice your shallow breathing, active mind, and muscle tension. This is your brain doing what it does best — keeping you safe (or at least, it thinks it is). You want to calm down, but you feel too worked up.

Dr. David Rock (2020) describes the SCARF model of human social experience, which runs on reward and threat responses in the brain. The five domains of threat and reward as described by Rock are:

Status: a sense of personal worth

Certainty: a sense of what the future holds

Autonomy: a sense of control over one's life

Relatedness: a sense of safety with others

Fairness: a sense of impartiality

This model describes the threat or reward responses that either push us away from something or draw us toward something.

These "five social domains activate the same threat and reward responses in our brain that we rely on for physical survival" (Mindtools, n.d.), and they happen subconsciously, before thought is ever activated. We release chemicals into our bloodstream as a stress reaction or a reward response.

Your brain is drawing people, places, and things toward you or pushing them away. This is the way God designed our brains.

The social domains are connected to trust, belonging, acceptance, and respect. We see this in everyday interactions with other humans. There are all kinds of ways we belong with a group or not with a group. Various attributes such as sex, outward appearance, political or religious affiliation, work teams, and social groups (e.g., sports team affiliation, clubs) are all areas or attributes of belonging.

But this makes the list of internal threats we can experience endless. We can trace much of what we feel about our place in a group back to our attachment as children (Siegel and Bryson, 2021). Many of us did not grow up with secure attachment, and this affects our view of the world and our safety in it. Those with insecure attachment may have a narrow window of tolerance and become triggered by threats more easily than those with secure attachment.

As I stated before, we were created to connect with and affect others.

You recognize this need to connect and affect, but you might wonder, "What does this have to do with how my brain works?" For now, I'd like us to focus on the survive region and the thrive region. We can actually detect when these areas activate on "functional MRI (fMRI) studies, which measure how neural activity changes blood flow, [allowing] neuroscientists and psychologists to witness the real-time working of the brain," (Chamine, 2012, p. 211).

The survive region of your brain is all about keeping you safe. It filters stimuli through a lens of fear. In the past, humans needed to run from lions and tigers and bears, but things are different now — sorta. People may no longer need to run from wild animals, but there are still threats out there, and they come from a variety of other sources, both internal and external, and all threats generate emotions.

The thrive region responds with more intention and is relational. It filters things that happen through love instead of fear. In the thrive region, we can handle life's challenges more effectively, without being swept away emotionally.

According to Chamine's positive intelligence framework (2012), which is a combination of neuroscience, positive psychology, cognitive behavioral science, and performance science, every thought, emotion, response, and reaction stems from the survive region or the thrive region.

When any of the SCARF domains become activated outside our window of tolerance, we can become dysregulated. When we're dysregulated, we instinctively have a fear-based reaction to the threat — a threat reaction — and we process this in the survive region. This is where our stress patterns jump into action.

The survive region is where your inner critic comes from, and like a gang leader it recruits allies — all your internal saboteurs.

When you are experiencing negative emotions such as condemnation and judgment, you're in the survive region. Don't be too hard on yourself — we all go there automatically when we feel threatened. But the difference between reacting out of the survive region and choosing to respond from the thrive region is learning to take a different pathway and then practicing that choice.

Stress patterns are your go-to reactions when you're outside your window of tolerance. These reactions are habitual and automatic.

Siegel and Bryson say that "neurons that fire together, wire together" (2014, p. 42). Think about dominos for a moment. One domino falls, and it begins a chain reaction. Over the decades of our lives, our brains have made more and more connections — more and more domino paths. The connections have to do with our upbringing, our environment, and our specific memories. These connections are all part of the chain reaction — the most preferred pathway — resulting in a response or a reaction to the stimuli.

Although we learn stress patterns in our youth, our brains can rewire, paving new pathways and making new connections. It's called neuroplasticity.

The thrive region consists of different, more positive pathways — for our purposes, coping mechanisms — creating limitless possibilities! They are "toward responses" instead of the "away responses" that we spoke of earlier.

In this region, you can "observe yourself, pause before acti[ng], soothe fear, [and] stay centered in the middle of [a] challenging situation and gut wisdom. ... We get to tap into the relational circuitry," which are the pathways that work together to help you tune in to the energy and emotions of others and yourself (Chamine, 2012, p.211-212).

We can use the relational circuitry to access various powers and be present or attuned to ourselves, others, and God. "As children, the strengths of our surviv[e] region and our thrive region are far more balanced than they are when we get older. As we grow up, our survive region is exercised, rewarded, and strengthened (Chamine, 2012), while the pathways of our thrive region are closed for construction. We create detours that bypass the pathways to the thrive region.

But it is when we are functioning in the thrive region we function best.

We get to bounce back and return to joy more quickly. This is not a Pollyanna, super-positivity mindset thing. It's taking captive our thoughts as we obey Christ (2 Corinthians 10:5). This is renewing our minds to be more in line with the One who created it. This is about being intentional — choosing pathways to the thrive region so you can tap into the limitless resources available to you.

As children, we are more present in the moment. We are open to possibilities and less limited by the internal chatter that consumes us as adults. As children, we can envision ourselves being the president of the United States or a professional golfer. We can dream and see things from perspectives that are not yet clear. We are unconsciously open to the possibilities of what God can actually do versus what we can do. As children, we love without bias and laugh and experience joy. As children, we don't take ourselves so seriously, and we trust in the One who knows better, saying if He says it, we believe it. This is a big faith.

As children, we create, innovate, and explore big visions and huge possibilities. We are overflowing with love, joy, and peace. We are super compassionate and moved by action. These are some things that are possible from the thrive region. I think Jesus said it best when He said, "Truly I tell you, unless you change and become like little children, you will never enter the kingdom of heaven. Therefore, whoever takes the lowly position of this child is the greatest in the kingdom of heaven. And whoever welcomes one such child in my name welcomes me" (Matthew 18:1-5). I'll leave this here for you to ponder, as you consider the qualities of the thrive region.

Part of living from the thrive region is learning to listen to the right voices. It is noticing what is happening in your body, which sends information to the brain, and quieting yourself in order to slow down and become intentional.

When we slow down enough, we get to listen to ourselves, others, and God at the withness level. This level of listening and understanding taps into the relational circuitry and stops the self-driven survival monster from taking charge.

From this place, we can learn how to be present for others, have joy while being present with them, and solve problems from a place of unity and teamwork.

It's this withness that becomes a witness of His love pouring out of you and through you. We are interconnected with others in humanity, fulfilling our purpose of being created for relationship.

Before we leave the two separate regions of the brain, I'd like for you to discover the difference between discernment and judgment and their relation to the two regions.

How do we know the difference between judgment and discernment? In the survive region, judgment lacks relational connection and joy. It is full of negative emotions, such as condemnation, fear, failure, and frustration.

Discernment is relational. It doesn't ignore problems with Pollyanna cliches, but it addresses them with the wisdom available in the thrive region. In this region, we can be courageous, calm, confident, and clear as we look at difficulties through the many powers available there. From this place of confidence and connection, we can address problems collaboratively, from a withness perspective instead of a combative, defensive reaction.

In defensive mode, one disconnects from the other person and focuses only on judging the problem and the person. When using discernment from the thrive region, one focuses on solving the problem with the other person and God. It's a withness thing; it's about connection.

One is problem-focused, and one is people-focused.

Maybe you recognize a pattern already. If so, chances are you are living exhausted and often feel empty. Chronically living with and reacting to low-level stress is draining your energy. Many of my clients report being depleted by the time they are ready to head home for the day, and there is nothing left to give to the people who are most important to them.

You no longer have to live like this because you can choose a different route. Start living in a place of love and abundance today. You can start responding to life intentionally instead of reacting automatically.

If you can't wait till this book develops to learn how this happens in your brain, please sign up for my free stress-shrinking playbook — 3 Ways to Shrink Your Stress & Exercise Your Brain — at https://www.doreensteenland.com/shrink-your-stress-playbook.

 **Mini Quiz**

Here's a little quiz for you.

Sit quietly and explore which region of your brain is ruling your life.

Do you do and say things to avoid emotional pain, later facing regret?

Do you do or say things to keep the peace, even when you have a different point of view?

Do you do or say things to gain the acceptance or appreciation of others?

Are you ruled with the desire to be perfect or near-perfect?

Do you over-function in the lives of others in order to be loved?

Do you jump in and take control of situations?

Do you feel you are always getting the bad breaks?

Do you feel the need to show people how much you know, but forget to show them how much you care?

If you said yes to any of these questions, you are most likely living from the survive region. This region is fear-based and desires to avoid pain at all costs; in reality, it's full of negative emotions, motives, and actions that make pain inevitable.

 **Withness Nugget:**

God desires for you to take your thoughts captive in obedience to Christ and renew your mind (2 Corinthians 10:5). God is active in the thrive region of your brain. This is where joy, connection, love, and all the fruit of the Spirit are produced. Dr. Allen Schore and Jim Wilder tell us, "Attachment develops through joy. When we are glad to be with someone, the energy of that joy strengthens our attachment. When we share joy, we become attached." Joy is relational. Relational joy builds attachments. We are happy to see one another. We rejoice when we are together. Joy is the celebration of attachment love. Schore explains that "joy builds identity and character in the brain. It is joy that gives us self-control. Joy is our strength. Joy lets us suffer well when we must suffer. This is *hesed* — secure attachment with joy. Joy and attachment provide powerful explanations for Jesus' character and victory" (Renovated, 2020, pg 76–77) (italics added).

Have you ever met a Christian that looks like they've been sucking on lemons? Yeah, you are not alone. This is a sign of a Christian who is dominated by his or her survive region. Little fruit, lots of judgment, many rules and regulations, duty upon duty, fear-based motivation, and legalism are survive region characteristics. Whole churches can run in survival mode because emotions — such as fear — are contagious. This is not how we are to show up as Christians, because this is not how God showed up for you. It is God's kindness and love that led you to change your ways (Romans 2), and love is not mandated by rules and regulations. Jesus was a perfect example of loving people where they are: accepting them; eating with them; washing their feet; serving them; discerning their hearts, needs, and motives; and modeling true love for them. They criticized Jesus for hanging with sinners and loving them unconditionally. Be like Jesus and love sinners unconditionally, even if you get criticized for it.

**Mindful Moments:**

Notice when your survive region has been activated today.

- What are the unique pathways that drive your fight, flight, freeze, or faint response?
- Notice any signals your body is sending you?
- What makes you want to escape this situation? Just get curious and notice today.

 **Journal Your Reflections:**

- Notice which region of your brain is dominant: love (thrive region) or fear (survive region)? Don't judge yourself — just notice.

- What do you want to be known for in your life?

- What is one small step you can take to shift away from cruise-control mode?

- Do you hide behind the constantly judging others and call it discernment?

- What patterns are you noticing? Reflect on your body and record any new sensations you notice, putting descriptive words on paper. Where in your body do you notice this sensation? Is there tension or weightlessness? Temperature changes? Is there a feeling or numbness? Notice your patterns from a place of curiosity — no judgment allowed.

## CHAPTER 5

# HOLY NOTICING: ATTENTION TO THE RIGHT THINGS

―――――♦―――――

Daily, external stimuli bombards our brains, including sounds. Like seismic sea waves traveling large spans of water, sound floods your brain. This sound demands your focus and directs your attention.

To ensure only the most important sounds get our focus, the brain has special neurons that act as gatekeepers, filtering out unimportant sounds so they don't reach the decision-making parts of the brain. These special neurons store information about patterns of sound, and these patterns enable us to predict what will happen next. Our brains love to predict, and these predictions allow us to narrow our attention, focus, and they start the subconscious habitual patterns into motion. But problems often arise when we place our attention in the wrong places.

Not only do our brains have to deal with incessant external sound, they have to deal with the internal voices* that speak to us inaudibly in our brains. Some of these voices are helpful. For instance, some help us memorize things and allow us to read silently. When we read silently, we are using our internal voices to "listen" to the words we are processing internally. We also use these internal voices to work through problems and come up with solutions as well as to motivate ourselves. Others actually sabotage us, such as our inner critic that finds the negative in everything.

Let's discuss the internal voices.

We listen to all kinds of voices, but the concept I want to draw your attention to is listening at a deep and intentional level. We need to discern — or notice with God— the right voices and silence the wrong ones. Let's just jump into a little background first.[2]

Your felt sense bears witness to what we already know — withness as a witness.

Romans 9:1 states, "I speak the truth in Christ — I am not lying, my conscience confirms it through the Holy Spirit — I have great sorrow and unceasing anguish in my heart."

---

[2] *For our purposes, we will not confuse these inner voices with auditory hallucinations — that is for psych 101. We're also not talking about our conscience, which is a separate inner voice that helps us determine right from wrong. When I say "inner voice(s)," I am specifically speaking of the internal chatter that provides us with information, whether accurate or inaccurate.

There are certain things we know to be true. We were created to have satisfying relationships with other humans and with God. God created special circuitry in our brains for this purpose. God also created the conscience to alert us to what's right and what's wrong. We each have an inner GPS that was written on our heart before the foundation of the world. The conscience is a gift from God. It is bigger than head knowledge and travels deeper to our heart, even to a sensory level. Some would say you can feel it. Now, as I say "feel it," the collective Christian community cringes in unison. We've been taught that feelings are dangerous, and the heart is deceitful (Jeremiah 17:9) and wicked (Genesis 6:5) and should be ignored. Yes, our feelings can be misguided; however, I believe the church has thrown the baby out with the bathwater. Your feelings provide data, and data begs to be explored.

God created the brain and designed how it works, and science is only just beginning to understand how this intricate mental computer system is wired and how it functions optimally.

fMRI equipment has allowed us to see how the brain's regions are both separate and linked. Like the map we discussed earlier, the pathways in the brain run through multiple regions and structures and become activated like a series of dominos by the trigger of the first domino. The impulse then travels the pathways, where energy is processed.

Where am I going with all this?

fMRI proves that emotions are real and processed via circuitry throughout our brains. So, if God created feelings, why are we so determined and go through so much trouble to numb, stuff, and deny them?

Didn't Adam and Eve *enjoy* God and *delight* in their relationship with Him as they walked in the garden?

If feelings were to be numbed, stuffed, and denied, why would Jesus weep?

Why would the psalms be full of rich and colorful emotion if feelings were to be crushed, killed, and destroyed?

As mentioned before, the brain will search for what it is looking for. So if you believe that feelings are wrong and sinful, your brain will look for evidence to confirm that belief. Your life will become very legalistic and performance-based, and then you certainly won't be bearing much fruit of the Spirit in your life.

When you intentionally numb negative feelings, you numb positive feelings — aka the fruit of the Spirit — as well. This leads to religion, duty, and performance instead of relationship with the Creator of the world. Sadly, this is the state of most mainstream churches today — lifeless and dull.

We can change this! God is about relationships, not religion. He actually condemned the religious leaders of the day and called them out as "blind guides" (Matthew 15:14, 23:16, 23:24).

What we need to understand is how to process our emotions and discern how to respond to them intentionally (thrive region) instead of automatically (survive region). I believe it is the automatic reactions to our emotions that entangle us in the place of sin that Christians so fear. It is these well-worn patterns of behavior that give feelings a bad rap in the church.

What if when we experienced our emotions, we could discern and run them through the region of the brain that taps into God's wisdom? Hang on, because this is where we are going, but not just yet.

Back to the voices. How do we discern these internal voices?

First, there is our conscience, which is written in our hearts and guides us in knowing right from wrong (Romans 2:15, 9:1, 14:23; 1 Kings 2:44). This conscience can become seared or dulled (1 Timothy 4:2). The conscience is what we sense deep down inside that can guide our behavior (if we are in tune to it, listen to it, and act according to what it is telling us!).

Next, we have our own inner voices. As previously explained, these have many functions. A variety of factors influence these voices, such as our attachments in childhood, our experiences, and sometimes the voices of those we perceive to be in authority in our lives. Some inner voices are helpful, while others are hurtful.

These inner voices drive our thoughts, feelings, and behaviors — most of the time subconsciously — so it comes down to which voices we listen to. The voices affect which pathways the stimuli is processed through — thrive or survive. Like the dominos, the voices set off a chain of events that lead us to our go-to pathways. These pathways lead to specific regions of the brain to set everything in motion.

Attachment is foundational to which voices we listen to. According to the four stages of the psychological theory of attachment, a child's experiences with his or her family of origin or immediate caregivers affect their perspectives and interactions with all aspects of life. Attachment is instinctive, and our initial relationships build the foundation for all our attachments, including our relationship with God (Ackerman, 2018).

We are created to be in connection with and to affect others. If we are nurtured in our earliest relationships, and that nurturing was reliable and consistent, we experienced secure attachment. We feel safe to explore the world because we subconsciously know we have a safe base to return to at any time. We more easily trust others because our caregivers have proven reliable and trustworthy. The relational circuitry is strong in this brain. Secure attachment is created with frequent eye contact; warm, engaging communication; empathetic concern; and connection. Studies have shown that even if a parent "flips their lid," repairing the rupture still leads to the formation of security. Of course ruptures in the relationship will happen; we will blow it as parents. Repairing those ruptures is key to empowering children to develop secure attachments. It also teaches them how to create and repair secure attachments with others with whom they are in relationship. As we connect with our kids, we affect them and create strong neural pathways.

If our earliest relationships are neglectful, unreliable, chaotic, or abusive, we develop stress patterns to survive and adapt to the lack of secure attachment. NOTE: Just realize that no matter how the survival pathways become your go-to for dealing with stress, you can break down the roadblocks to your thrive circuitry!

The strongest force in the human brain is attachment. Jesus, with His human brain perfectly attached to His Father, actively resisted temptation and gained victory over sin. "Attachment develops through joy. When we are truly glad to be with someone, the energy of that joy strengthens our attachment. When we share joy, we become attached." (Wilder (quoting a conversation with Schore), 2020, p. 76).

"Neurotheology has debated for decades whether there is a "God receptor" somewhere in the nervous system" (Wilder, 2020, p. 79). When we think "with God" — withness as a witness — and actively pursue a relationship with our Creator, we can become of mutual mind with God in the thrive region. We have just scratched the surface in the study of neurotheology, and fMRI findings indicate that the thrive region lights up with all things spiritual. It would also tell us we can access the root of our essence and character in the thrive region (Wilder, 2020, p. 79). Again, we must connect in the relational circuitry to affect others from this withness space.

 **Withness Nugget:**

What if God is not as angry as some taught us in Sunday School?

What if God delights in you more than you can imagine? The God of the universe created you and delights in you — in all of you! The messy parts of you that have not yet been sanctified are priceless to Him. He delights in using all your mess to create a message that is uniquely yours. There is no one else like you. No one can do what you were put on this earth to accomplish.

The world has tainted your inner voices, but now it is time to step into your power and holy notice His voice! The world loves to distract, yet He asks us to go deeper still. It is in the stillness that we attune ourselves to Him and His direction. We get to listen to His voice and connect our minds with His. In this space, we find the mind and heart of God. We have access to the fruit of His Spirit because we are attached to and identified in and through Him. "'For in him we live and move and have our being.' As some of your own poets have said, 'We are his offspring'" (Acts 17:28).

When we connect to our source, we can love — because God is love. He delights in you; He sings over you; and He created you in His image (Zephaniah 3:17; Genesis 1:27). This attachment does not come through rules and regulations but through attachment love. Dr. Wilder and Dr. Warner would argue that this love is a combination of *hesed* and *agape*, and it is defined as attachment love. I love the way the Amplified Bible interprets 1 John 4:18: "There is no fear in love [dread does not exist]. But perfect [complete, full-grown] love drives out fear because fear involves [the expectation of divine] punishment, so the one who is afraid [of God's judgment] is not perfected in love [has not grown into a sufficient understanding of God's love]."

 **Mindful Moments:**

Practice breathing deeply. Notice the air going in and out of your lungs. Notice the temperature of the air as it enters your nostrils and the temperature of the air as it exits them. Rest for a moment in His presence and listen deeply for His loving words, as words of condemnation do not come from Him. He is a God who comforts you with His presence and guides you in your next best steps. He is with you. Notice His presence. Feel it fully. Be embraced by His warmth and consider the way He delights in you. Allow yourself to bask in the emotion of being known intimately by the Risen King. Experience the fruit of the Spirit: love, joy, peace, patience, kindness, goodness, faithfulness, gentleness, and self-control (Galatians 5:22-23) — but not from a theological standpoint! Don't define them. Feel them and sit in those feelings. God is right next to you and is delighting in your time of rest in Him.

**Journal Your Reflections:**

- What did you holy notice as you rested in His presence?
- How can you attune your ears to His voice today? Notice if the internal chatter is positive or negative. Get curious about this.
- What emotion was off-limits for you as a child? Get curious about this. What was wrong with that emotion? After reading the examples above, is that an accurate assessment or a lie you have been living by?
- You cannot selectively numb emotions. If you are trying to numb negative emotions, you will also numb the positive ones, i.e., the fruit of the Spirit. What new awareness are you having as you ponder this truth?
- What patterns are you noticing? Reflect on your body and record any new sensations you notice, putting descriptive words on paper. Where in your body do you notice this sensation? Is there tension or weightlessness? Temperature changes? Is there a feeling or numbness? Notice your patterns from a place of curiosity — no judgment allowed.

CHAPTER 6

# ON THE ROAD

---◆---

You've planned your route; you know where the construction is and do your best to avoid the construction. The fact remains that construction is always part of the ride — but we get to choose how we navigate it.

When our time on the road is uneventful, we enjoy a serene and harmonious experience. Something about driving under these conditions expands and opens up your thinking. Ever notice how it's kind of like the shower? When you get in the shower or when you're having an uneventful drive, ideas and possibilities suddenly come to you. It's as if this space created room to breathe, be, and think clearly. This is because your brain has entered what Dr. Daniel Siegel calls the window of tolerance. This is the space where we are in the optimal zone of arousal.

In this imaginary window, you experience the light and a gentle breeze. This window is spotless, allowing you to see through it clearly. The colors are vibrant when looking through this window, and you appreciate the moment and experience your surroundings. A sense of harmony fills the air as the relaxing rhythm of life unfolds around you. From within this space, we get to make meaning of our circumstances, regulate our emotions, and experience them to the full.

When in this window, it's like a beautiful orchestra (Betz, 2019). All the instruments are playing together, in harmony; each separate, but linked (Siegel, 2020b). The sound is crisp, complex, full, and beautiful. There is immense enjoyment, and positive emotion results as you experience the music. Your body senses the vibrations of the music, and you may get goosebumps or feel tears well up in your eyes because of the beauty of the sound. At this moment, you are completely in the present, enjoying the performance. There is harmony, joy, peace, and glee as you are in your optimal zone of arousal — energized as you flow with the music. There is balance and stability, despite the changing movements of the score. Immersed in the moment, we notice the individual parts working together.

Now imagine you are in this window, listening to beautiful music, when suddenly one instrument plays the wrong note or loses the beat. All your attention turns to what is out of place — the sound that doesn't belong. The same error detection system that activates to the wrong note is the same one that lights up when stressful stimuli enter the scene.

When you're in the window, all the parts are integrated, working together in harmony. When outside the window, integration is temporarily impaired; hyperarousal and hypoarousal are more likely to prevail (Siegel, n.d.). A hyper- or hypoarousal state is a reaction when the nervous system detects and calculates a threat (real or imagined) and we become dysregulated. This is an automatic reaction, and we all experience these little nervous system "pokes" all day long.

When we are flexible, adaptable, coherent, energized, and stable (FACES) (Siegel & Bryson, 2019), we are responding from an integrated brain — the many parts of the brain are working together in a coordinated and balanced fashion. We can think clearly and appreciate what is happening in the moment, noticing that we have departed the window and then self-regulating to get back in it. Self-regulation is the key to being in the window of tolerance. During a moment of stress — when threatened or triggered — we are able to remain in or depart only temporarily from our window of tolerance, avoiding dysregulation.

However, when we leave the window of tolerance and become emotionally dysregulated, we default to our stress patterns. Stress patterns are like well-worn roadways riddled with construction and traffic jams. When dysregulated, we can become stuck in the resulting chaos or rigidity. Stress patterns are our old ways of managing dysregulation and can include multiple defenses (Hendel, 2018). When a person moves outside the window and experiences difficulty regulating emotionally, this person may "feel rigid [or] numb[,] or emotions might flood the [person's brain] with chaos" (Siegel, 2020b, p. 347); it depends on where your nervous system takes you — fight, flight, freeze/faint, or fawn. Think of your nervous system as the GPS trying to pick the route it thinks will best keep you safe.

For those who have experienced trauma — 50% of all people — flowing outside the window occurs more easily and therefore more frequently, and they have a more difficult time self-regulating. They often feel out of control or anxious, as the stimuli "bombards the[ir] mind[,] affecting [] rational thinking and social behavior" (Siegel, 2020b, p. 347).

The good news is, we can grow our ability to use the right coping mechanisms, increasing the size of the window. Research has shown that those who have experienced trauma have a narrow window of tolerance. The goal of expanding the window of tolerance is improving our ability to regulate our brains and body, so we can bounce back from setbacks quickly and live a balanced life. We can enjoy a harmonious life instead of a stressed-out, frazzled state of being.

When harmony is disrupted, many factors (which we will discuss later) influence the stress patterns you typically experience during travel.

When you hit construction, you are unstable internally, being "tossed back and forth by the waves" (Ephesians 4:1). All you want is control and/or stability, so you resort to stress patterns that your brain has categorized as the best route to safety. Even if those patterns are no longer serving you, they feel familiar and provide the illusion of control. We will explore different stress patterns later; but for now, what I'd like you to notice is that reactions are often extreme. Harmony — balance in our brain — is the ability to achieve emotional stability and regulate our brain and body.

"[E]motion, meaning making, and social interactions are mediated through the [] relational circuitry in the brain" (Siegel,

2020b, p. 348). When this circuitry is in play, we have full access to the accelerator and the braking mechanism in our brain. When we have full access to acceleration and braking, we can respond instead of react. This full access is being in the window of tolerance.

When we leave the window of tolerance, the voices of our saboteurs are amplified. These voices affect all aspects of our life. Dr. Daniel Amen calls them ANTs — automatic negative thoughts — and they can influence our decisions on where to go. These negative thoughts come in all shapes and sizes, and it's possible you have go-to ANTs as well as go-to saboteurs.

Some of these ANTs are:

All-or-nothing thinking (aka black-and-white thinking): everything is completely good or completely bad; it shows up with words such as always, never, should, and shouldn't.

Fortunetelling: predicting a poor outcome in the future; e.g., "I'm going to fail, then my kid will be homeless and lying in a ditch…."

Blaming: a shame-based reaction that looks to shift responsibility for a poor result to someone who does not actually own responsibility for the result.

Mind reading: assuming that you can read someone else's heart and thoughts, without asking them.

Magnification (aka catastrophizing): when the importance of an incident is exaggerated.

These are just a few ANTs that can appear when we leave the window of tolerance. These thoughts fuel reactivity and can become a vicious cycle. It's like taking an offramp to make a U-turn, only to jump on the next offramp and repeat the process indefinitely. This cyclical thinking makes us feel trapped and stuck, yet somehow our brains trick us into believing this solves our problem.

I'd like you to step into intention. Begin to notice what is happening inside and outside as you approach the construction zone. Get curious, without judgment, exploring what's keeping you stuck. What are you seeing? What are you feeling? What are you hearing? Perhaps, right now, it's like the radio is playing, but there is static and noise. What would it look like to tune in to the calming voice of God instead of amplifying the static? Are you able to attune yourself to *the* voice of calm? If not, can you ground yourself with breathing exercises and restabilize until you can?

The good news is that every human can expand their window of tolerance and live a more harmonious life. We will discover how we can detect, or holy notice, when we are entering a construction zone by observing what is happening within us. The signs are subtle. The energy of emotions and the tension throughout the body are the telltale signs. If we can self-regulate, we can effortlessly bounce back to the peaceful flow within the window of tolerance.

When we are in the window of tolerance, we are able to cling to God when we begin to see the "construction ahead" signs. This connection with God increases our stability and fruitfulness in the middle of our construction-zone moments.

John 15:1-17:

I am the true vine, and my Father is the gardener. [2] He cuts off every branch in me that bears no fruit, while every branch that does bear fruit he prunes so that it will be even more fruitful. ³ You are already clean because of the word I have spoken to you. ⁴ Remain in me, as I also remain in you. No branch can bear fruit by itself; it must remain in the vine. Neither can you bear fruit unless you remain in me. I am the vine; you are the branches. If you remain in me and I in you, you will bear much fruit; apart from me, you can do nothing. … ⁸ This is to my Father's glory, that you bear much fruit, showing yourselves to be my disciples. "As the Father has loved me, so have I loved you. Now remain in my love. ¹⁰ If you keep my commands, you will remain in my love, just as I have kept my Father's commands and remain in his love. ¹¹ I have told you this so that my joy may be in you and that your joy may be complete. ¹² My command is this: Love each other as I have loved you. … ¹⁷ This is my command: Love each other.

We produce fruit when we stay connected with Him within the window of tolerance. We cannot bear the fruit of the Spirit when we disconnect from God.

Sometimes we need pruning to produce fruit. Pruning can be painful, but it promises fruit production. Growth does not happen without difficulty and discomfort. Consider what old stress patterns need to be pruned for fresh growth to occur.

When we remain in love (God is love) — that is, stay connected — we experience joy completely, regardless of the pruning difficulties. We see the gifts and opportunities that come from being pruned. Fresh growth always comes.

When we remain in love, we can bear much fruit. The fruit of the Spirit is love, joy, peace, patience, kindness, goodness, faithfulness, gentleness, and self-control. This is the ultimate goal.

### Withness Nugget:

Immanuel, God is with you. He is with you in your moments of dysregulation, so don't resort to your old lone ranger ways. You are not alone. He desires for you to live in harmony with Him — think vine and branches. This is where we get to process life with Him from a space of stability.

God designed your brain to be flexible, adaptable, coherent, energized, and stable. You get to choose how to step into this power that He has already provided for you. You have everything you need to expand your window of tolerance and grow in your connection with Christ. I realize this is easier said than done, but you can choose to rewire the patterns in your brain and shift into this space of calm connection.

Visualize yourself integrated within yourself and with God. Notice the peace and feel the safety. You can relax knowing you are cared for perfectly. You are connected, and nothing can separate you from Him who is in you. Rest in this truth right now — He will never leave you. Sit back and enjoy the gentle ride of peace that passes understanding (Philippians 4:7).

### Mindful Moments:

Use your discernment and practice this only if you feel you have the resources at this moment, staying connected to God as you visualize. See yourself in your stress pattern. Step back and visualize it like a film. What do you see? What do you smell? What do you feel, and where in your body do you feel it? Can you label it?

Shift yourself back into the window with Him. Take a few deep breaths, and then gently rub two fingertips together with enough pressure that you notice all the sensations. Now, visualize yourself with the One who is peace and love. It is peaceful and calm. What do you see? What do you smell? What do you feel in your body, and where do you feel it? Can you label it?

 **Journal Your Reflections:**

- What circumstances propel you to disconnect and dysregulate? Be very specific about your answer, and try to discover what patterns you might notice.
- When dysregulated, what pattern kicks in for you (people pleasing, perfectionism, control, avoidance, victimhood, etc.)?
- What needs to happen for you to stay connected despite your dysregulation?
- What patterns are you noticing? Reflect on your body and record any new sensations you notice, putting descriptive words on paper. Where in your body do you notice this sensation? Is there tension or weightlessness? Temperature changes? Is there a feeling or numbness? Notice your patterns from a place of curiosity — no judgment allowed.

CHAPTER 7

# CHANGING YOUR ROUTE ON THE FLY

———◆———

I live in New Jersey, and driving here requires advanced skills. Aggressiveness is a learning objective for our teens as they prepare to drive — it's a survival tactic for the highway on-ramps. We train them that if you don't put yourself out there, you can never enter the roadway. Like most highways, the speed limit is 65 miles per hour and the left lane is for passing. Also like most highways, those who wish to travel above the speed limit use the left lane. And we've all seen or heard of the people who get road rage if you're going 65 mph in this lane — New Jersey has a lot of them!

Daily as we travel this highway, we see drivers who flip their lids. They not only drive aggressively — which is dangerous — but they drive vindictively! You see them in the rearview mirror, in a huge SUV, apparently unconcerned they're about to drive right over you. You look to get out of their path, but sometimes there is no escape. At this moment, your heart rate rises, your breathing shallows, and you become hyper-focused on survival. The situation compels you to speed up or risk being run over, so you speed up. Your tension escalates as you see the smoke coming out of the other driver's ears. They're tailgating you, driving what appears to be inches from your bumper. If you don't move fast enough for them, they flash their high beams and beep their horns. Your brain is only aware of the imminent threat and will respond in one of four ways: fight, flight, freeze/faint, or fawn mode.

The first reaction in this moment could be fight. In this mode, you become confrontational and react aggressively (or passive aggressively). Maybe you tap your brakes to taunt them to hit you, or maybe you slow down even more. Yikes! These are never a good plan. These reactions throw fuel on the fire, occasionally turning tragic. The SUV might escalate from there, crossing four lanes over to the right lane, speeding up to 90 mph, then darting across four lanes again to get in front of you. It's quite the sight as you brace for a collision.

You may not be overtly aggressive with your driving, but you do scream in your car at the offender. As a people watcher, I find it fascinating to see the different ways people flip their lid. (Full disclaimer: I have flipped my lid. I have hurled condemning verbal bullets. Sadly, this was in front of my kids.) Being aggressive in the face of a threat is an automatic reaction for many of us, especially if the possibility of an actual confrontation with the threat is near zero.

The next reaction is flight. This is where you get out of the big SUV's way as soon as possible, totally removing yourself from the threatening situation. This is a high-energy state, and you may have anxiety and panic as you try to avoid any confrontation. You immediately hope to get away, so you withdraw from or yield to the threat, often stuffing your emotions. I've done this too, especially when I'm already drained of energy. Perhaps I'm hungry, angry, lonely, tired, or overwhelmed and just cannot fight the battle. I pull over to get out of the way, most times annoying the people in the next lane, and yet I'm unable to relieve my stress reaction even though the threat no longer exists.

The third potential reaction is freezing/fainting.* I've noticed this one most frequently in new drivers and older adults. They become confused and slow down, further increasing the risk of accident on this superhighway. Shutting down is a low-energy response. They don't know what to do next, so they freeze like a deer in headlights.

The fourth potential reaction to this threat is a learned pattern of appeasing called fawning.+ This is when you get out of the way and apologize by waving or lip-synching "I'm sorry" through the window. You feel guilty that you inconvenienced the other driver and often overthink the situation. This can show up in all kinds of stress patterns, including people-pleasing and taking responsibility (or blame) for something that is not your fault. You aren't thinking about your own needs or experience; instead, you cater to everyone else's. You aspire to be sure that the mad driver likes you before passing by. This reaction is a survival tactic to remain safe and regain balance. This response is most often seen in those who are recovering from trauma, this is a learned and blended state in the nervous system.

Driving in New Jersey (or anywhere) can be risky business! And these same kinds of threats — real or perceived — happen in your brain daily.

The window of tolerance is a place of harmony and thriving. Think Goldilocks and the three bears — everything is "just right" (or easily made so).

The Goldilocks principle of stress and anxiety is the optimal zone where you perform your best. Performance science has shown that you need some stress to perform well, otherwise you reach boredom. But there is a tipping point for everyone; it's at that point a person has left the window of tolerance and performance declines.

When we are in the window of tolerance, we are calm, confident, focused, creative, and have great clarity. If we are unable to bounce back quickly when we leave this window, things get fuzzy, and then we fall back on some of our survival reactions.

Now, just to be clear: We all flow in and out of this window all day long. Staying in this window 24/7 is unrealistic given all the various stimuli we are exposed to on a daily basis. There are two things I'd like you to consider. First, if you have experienced trauma in the past, you have a narrow window of tolerance, which means you flow out of it more easily (and therefore more frequently) than others. Second, we can expand this window through neuroplasticity, thus increasing our resilience. We can bounce back into our window of tolerance and return to harmony, attuned to others in our environment.

There are three possibilities when we move outside the window of tolerance: hyperarousal (chaos), hypoarousal (rigidity), or bounce back. Fight and flight reactions result from hyperarousal, and freeze/faint result from hypoarousal. The fawn reaction is a blend which leads us into Stephen Porges Polyvagal Ladder.+

Our goal is to bounce back quickly instead of remaining in the dysregulated state — this is resilience. When we are in the window, we are present, engaged, and connected with others, ourselves, and God, and we don't react at all — we respond. This is the work: to notice when you've left the window and regulate your emotions so that you can return to joy and peace by being present, engaged, and connected with yourself, others, and God — to respond and not react. Just a quick note to say, you cannot jump from dysregulated to peace immediately. I wish you could. There is a hierarchy, or order, that the nervous system becomes regulated according to Polyvagal theory – you don't skip rungs on the ladder, you must climb up the ladder – this is normal. Your window of tolerance can be expanded and you can learn to shift into different states of being – regaining control of your inner world –one rung on the ladder at a time.

---

*Since fainting is more of a medical emergency, we will not focus our attention here.

+The fawn reaction is an adaptive, blended state involving the ventral vagal branch of the nervous system that activates in response to neuroception—your brain's unconscious system for detecting safety or threat. When your nervous system senses potential relational danger, social rejection, or conflict, it may instinctively move into appeasement to maintain connection and prevent harm. This is often a trauma-based response learned over time.

However, not all blended states indicate trauma. Some are healthy and reflect flexible engagement. The key question is: Where is this behavior coming from? Are you pleasing others from an underlying fear—an attempt to create internal safety—or from a grounded, conscious choice aligned with your values? Is your "yes" a full-bodied, regulated response—or a nervous system's survival strategy?

 **Managing Your Window of Tolerance**

Notice the following internal states when you go into the hypoarousal zone, the hyperarousal zone, and the optimal zone in the window of tolerance. Get very specific so that you can notice in real time and bounce back quickly.

What do you notice about your thinking?

What do you notice when you feel stressed out?

What does your body feel?

What do you impulsively turn toward during discomfort?

If **dysregulated**, what do you see at this moment
(look at your present surroundings and use your visual cues to reground yourself)?

What do you hear
(listen for sounds closest to you and furthest away)?

What words can you put to your experience?
I feel (emotion). I am sensing in my body (sensations), and it reminds me of (title only; no details). I am here and now in the present, and I can use (tool) to self-regulate in this moment.

## YOUR MIRROR NEURONS AND WHY THEY MATTER

Your brain houses special mirror neurons. What makes them different is that these neurons can mimic and execute both motor and sensory stimuli that are observed. The "mirror neurons respond only to an act with intention, where there's some predictability or purpose that can be perceived."(Siegel & Bryson, 2012, p. 124). These neurons were a gift from God to allow us to connect relationally with ourselves, others, and God. These neurons assist us in connecting with others by showing empathy and responding compassionately. They are how we feel the energy and emotion of others — they create a type of social and emotional contagion, playing a part in how we monitor and interpret the actions of others and ourselves. They connect you to the relational circuitry in the brain (Kilner & Lemon, 2013).

Researchers hypothesize that some autistic people lack connections between these super-important cells in their brain, while highly sensitive people have more active mirror neurons than the average person, thus allowing them to feel and absorb emotion at a higher rate and intensity.

A simple example of mirror neurons sensing and performing motor abilities without our consent would be when you are in a meeting and someone yawns, then everyone yawns. This is physical contagion.

Another common example of mirror neurons at work with emotions is when there's a general mood that affects everyone in a room. When there is joy or delight in the room, it's amazing to see this spread! However, when there is anger, resentment, or other negative emotion in the room, it's not so amazing.

Emotional contagion is a fact, and how we manage this contagion depends on which region we activate.

For example, if large amounts of negative emotion are being generated in a room, mirror neurons will jump on the bandwagon — unless directed by the brain to show up differently. The way mirror neurons react is called resonance. This resonance syncs us to others by mirroring the contagious emotion.

In the workforce, emotional contagion influences a company's culture. For example, Apple has structured its company around innovation and collaboration. They live it and model it; it is the culture's contagion. The cool thing about this is that Apple's two foundational values originate in the thrive region instead of the survive region. This generates more of a growth mindset in their environment, as opposed to a fixed mindset that fears failure.

For those of you in management or responsible for team building, the culture you create is contagious — your results will flow from the culture you build. Your employees' job satisfaction, loyalty to your vision, and level of engagement all begin with the culture you reflect — and how you communicate your vision and build a sense of connection, appreciation, and gratitude, originating in the thrive region of your brain.

We can observe the implication of emotional contagion in any organization of human beings. Think about our education system, our medical system, our government, and our law enforcement branches. The culture and the happiness in these systems are all affected by mirror neurons. Author Simon Sinek, in his book "Start with Why" (2011), does a great job discussing how to affect organizations and have people move together as a team. For our purposes, I'd like us to focus on the neuroscience aspect and impact of your mirror neurons on your world!

We were made to connect with others, and your mirror neurons guarantee that will happen. The question is, will you connect with negativity or with positivity? This question will guide your happiness and your success in whatever environment you find yourself in.

With activated mirror neurons, you quickly follow the actions and attitudes that are present in your environment. If your negative emotions are charged, you enter your survive region. If your emotions are positive, you process them in the thrive region. For now, let's focus on negative emotions.

When a negative emotion reveals itself in a group or community and activates your survive region, your defenses jump into action. These defenses manifest themselves in 10 different signature patterns according to how you learned to survive and function in your childhood — based on your environment and what your family modeled for you. These defenses served you well for years, but they have outstayed their welcome.

We will do an analysis of these signature patterns — aka "saboteurs" — in the next two chapters; for now, notice how these mirror neurons affect connection, empathy, and the ability to interpret what others are experiencing. These neurons activate your withness — where you resonate with others and your world becomes bigger than just yourself.

In this moment, your brain will choose the pathway to react or respond from. These pathways are love- or fear-based, and in that space we get to notice with God, or pause. There is so much power in the pause. With our pause, we are able to notice what is happening within us and around us and make better choices. We no longer need to be held captive by our automatic reactions.

Between stimulus and response, there is a space due to the micro delay between the fast and slow tracks in the brain; this offers us a moment of choice, or a pause. It is here that we get to flex our mental muscles, choosing to respond instead of reacting.

It is during this pause that we get to choose: Do we stay on "Route Survive" or take the exit onto "Route Thrive"? If we stay on Route Survive, we remain disconnected from those around us and react from fear-based patterns. The problem becomes more important than the person, and the relationship is sacrificed for perceived logic. This is where we usually make our decisions based on fear, in the part of the brain that has a programmed way of solving problems. When the brain takes these pathways and actions, they are not innovative or creative.

If we choose the exit to Route Thrive, there will be a sense of withness and teamwork as we solve problems in a relational way. On Route Thrive, we become curious and open to creative thinking. We listen to understand and connect rather than just fix. We see things in a positive light as we discover creative solutions and look at the big picture. When we choose this pathway, we can activate all kinds of possibilities. As you consider this, you have a choice: stay on the pathway to disconnection or take the ramp to connection.

This holy-noticing moment — the space between the circumstance and reacting or responding — is where you get to choose. Now, this superhighway allows you to pause, take some deep breaths, and check your map. This is the moment of decision, and it happens in a nanosecond. If left unsupervised, your brain will go into protection and survival mode. It will actively try to solve the problem, disregarding the relationship in front of you. This is where you analyze and judge your circumstances, often with highly charged negative emotions.

This is your chance to shift — to pause, breathe, and choose relationship and love. You get to choose if you will turn toward God and an openhearted response of love, or allow your stress patterns to dictate that you take the road of disconnection, fear, and judgment.

This is your withness moment — where you can call on God and His power, love, and grace to infuse your situation.

One last thought about stress. There is a difference between "threat stress and challenge stress." Threat stress is what we are describing above. Challenge stress is what we need in order to maintain an interest in new and difficult things we try to do (Epel, 2022). In my groups, we call these stretches, because we are stretching outside our comfort zone. Now, we are not so far out of our comfort zone that we become dysregulated. We go outside our comfort zone just enough to stretch our thinking and our pathways in order to learn new ways of functioning.

Think through this for a moment. When you were a child learning to ride a bike, it was a stretch. You were learning a new skill. There was a risk of falling, yet you did it. By learning to ride a bike, you paved new pathways in your brain. This is challenge stress, and it's healthy. Sometimes we react to challenge stress as if it is threat stress. We must properly identify the type of stress we are experiencing in the moment. When we correctly identify the type of stress, we realize that "failure is part of success[,] and you cannot have success without failure. This takes the threat out of [challenge] stress when we see failures as a byproduct of challenging ourselves to stretch" (Epel, 2022, p. 70). Our best selves emerge when we experience the right stress. If we see all stress as threat stress, we cannot learn when we're being stretched.

 **Withness Nugget:**

Special mirror neurons allow us to connect with other humans. They allow us to experience emotion, empathetically and compassionately.

Wilder et al. talk about a joy center being activated as a "happy to be with you" response. This is when you are in the relational circuitry of the brain and you connect with the other human(s) in your presence. This is where people become more important than any problems. The relational circuitry empowers us to be present and engaged with other human beings.

Remember who you are — you are a child of the King, created in His image to do good works that were predetermined before the foundation of the world (Ephesians 2:10). You have a purpose that only you can accomplish on this earth. You were created to connect and affect others (Genesis 2:18) — you were created for community. In order to connect in your community, you must get relational and put aside the flesh, which wars to be first. Get comfortable being uncomfortable.

A friendly reminder about the above verse. This took place in a garden, so get out in nature with others and worship the Creator of all creation. Look upon humanity and all that God created with awe and wonder, and tap into the gratitude and joy He desires for us to experience. Focus on the "glimmers" that God has provided for us. "Glimmers are micro-moments of harmony that appear every day but often go unnoticed. When we begin to appreciate these glimmers, we can shape our nervous system toward wholeness and well-being" (Dana, 2021,pp 92).

**Mindful Moments:**

In this pause, feel your feet on the ground. Breathe deeply or sigh. Notice what you discover. What energy shifts are you sensing in this moment?

"A sigh has been called the 'resetter' of our nervous system. We can use intentional sighing as a way to interrupt our state and find a momentary reset and also to deepen an experience of regulation and connection" (Deb Dana, 2021, p117). According to Dana, there are basic ways we sigh. "We sigh with frustration to release some energy, and we sigh when we feel down or depressed in order to bring in some energy. We sigh in relief as we find our way back to regulation, and then breathe a sigh of contentment to savor the experience of being safely anchored there" (Dana, 2021 pg. 118).

 **Journal Your Reflections:**

- What have you noticed about emotional contagion in your own life?
- What is the energy you experience in your body as emotional contagion?
- When have you noticed someone's face light up to see you? How did that feel? What was your response?
- What was the flavor of that conversation?
- How can you look at mankind and God's creation from a fresh light of gratitude and appreciation? We are all humans sharing this planet together — look at it all with love.
- What biases might be keeping you stuck in your same old patterns?
- What patterns are you noticing? Reflect on your body and record any new sensations you notice, putting descriptive words on paper. Where in your body do you notice this sensation? Is there tension or weightlessness? What temperature changes do you notice?

## CHAPTER 8

# LANE CLOSURES AHEAD (THE EXPRESS HIGHWAY TO POSSIBILITY)

---

For competitive golfers, a stroke play tournament of any kind comes with a love–hate relationship. When all is going well, it's easy-peasy; but when the wheels come off the bus, it becomes incredibly stressful. Managing your inner world is imperative for playing good golf, and it is a learned skill.

During one of my tournaments, I was on a par 5 hole, which means it takes the average person five shots to get the ball in the hole. Anything less is great; anything more does not feel so good.

This specific hole had a large pond in front of the green. The sound of the water trickling over the stones was mesmerizing. It was a beautiful day. The skies were blue, and the grass was a vivid green. As I took my shot, my contact was poor, and the ball went in the water. My brain shifted into panic mode, because I had placed great importance on this tournament. I felt the heat traveling up my spine to my head. Shame swirled in my mind. I entered judgment mode as my inner critic pounced on me, screaming its head off. The skies lost their vivid color and everything appeared much darker, but of course the actual weather was not the culprit. I hurried to escape the shame and condemnation of my inner critic and repeated the mistake several times in a row. For the golfers out there, it was a "Tin Cup" moment — I was no longer in control of my actions. When you are in this threat state, your only goal is escaping the threat. Your neurotransmitters emit an array of powerful activating chemicals that tighten your muscles, raise your blood pressure and heart rate, and narrow your vision. Your breathing also becomes shallow and quick, and the thinking portion of your brain shuts off to send energy to the muscles in the body. I was smack dab in the middle of a high-alert situation. Think escape, run for your life — survival mode — because that's what I was thinking. In reality, it was just an imperfect shot, and I should have recognized it as challenge stress and been able to move forward with clarity and focus — but that is not what happened.

It triggered me! This is a real concept, and we each face our own triggers every day. These triggers set off a chain reaction in your brain. If you do not intercept this reaction and return to the window of tolerance — your home base for harmony — you will follow the most traveled pathway in your brain. This pathway is different for everyone, but it usually shows up as our "favorite" saboteurs.

Your brain is a connecting machine. The trigger occurs when your brain connects your current circumstance(s) to the feelings, judgments, thoughts, and beliefs associated with the memories of previous life experiences. These internal connections may or may not be accurate, but they begin the chain reaction. Your brain does not know the difference between a genuine threat and a perceived threat. Your brain is reacting to data that can be real, imaginary, or misinterpreted.

The data you uncover can be useful in intercepting the triggered reaction. The good news is that you no longer need to be tossed back and forth by every triggering experience! You can choose to travel on Route Thrive. Choosing the thrive pathways is remapping your brain! Instead of automatically reacting out of the survive region, you'll widen and repave your thrive pathways so that they become your automatic response.

What if you framed all the energy that came into your body from the outside world as data that needs to be evaluated? The energy from people, places, and things that enter your body from the external world is trying to gain your attention. This energy jumps into motion and travels through your brain and body like a wildfire travels through the woods. You can strengthen your neural pathways so that you can notice the direction the fire is traveling. The more you observe, the more you can consciously select the path to follow — you become the wind, directing the flames and controlling the energy's route.

When we are not mindful, we are reactive. Reactivity is the marker of saboteur activity and survival mode. We will explore these patterns of reactivity, because when we "name it, we can tame it" (Siegel & Bryson, 2012, p. 27).

Let's first explore the role of saboteurs as described by Shirzad Chamine in "Positive Intelligence" (2012). The saboteurs live in the survive region and jump to your defense to solve problems and get needs met in the most expedient and "safe" (as far as they're concerned) manner. Many factors affect the development of these saboteurs in childhood, think attachment theory–a foundational concept in Interpersonal Neurobiology. These saboteurs were essential for keeping us safe and meeting our needs, ultimately defining our identity. Instead of fostering creativity and innovation, these saboteurs undermine our confidence. They drive a wedge between us and others, fostering disconnection and disengagement. We're fooled into thinking we have control, but we're actually held captive by these screaming inner voices. They are thieves that rob us of joy and peace in our lives and keep us in the status quo. The result is a life that feels mundane, exhausting, and unsatisfying. These saboteurs do not need to be allowed to take charge. We can intercept their power (Frey, 2022)!

There is a battle raging in our minds between myriad voices from the two regions of the brain. Chamine calls the ones from our survive region our internal enemies, or saboteurs. "These saboteurs each have their own set of automatic, habitual pattern loops. They each have their own beliefs, their own voice, and their own assumptions" (Chamine, 2012, pp. 16-17).

We all have saboteurs; the only question is how much control they have in our minds. These "saboteurs developed in early childhood to survive perceived threats of life, both physical and emotional. By the time we are adults, these saboteurs are no longer needed" (Chamine, 2012, p. 16-17), but they have become our invisible influencers. The stronger these saboteurs are in our lives, the wider the automatic survive pathways are in our brains. Big roads handle traffic with efficiency, which means they become your default route to your destination. The same holds true for your patterns of behavior. You can learn to intercept your automatic pathways and choose a different route.

The gang of invisible influencers is squatting on your land, but you can reclaim your territory. Here's a brief introduction to these saboteurs. We will focus on the primary culprit first, then dive into the rest later. The primary culprit for almost everyone is "the Judge," or as many like to call it, the inner critic.

This menacing influencer finds fault with all the people, places, and things in your life, including yourself. "It generates much of your anxiety, stress, anger, disappointment, shame and guilt. Its self-justifying lie is that without it, you or others would turn into lazy and unambitious beings who would not achieve much. Its voice is often mistaken as a tough love voice of reason" (Chamine, 2012, p. 17). Let's just call it what it is: judgment that stems from a fear-based, performance-based, fixed mindset. It no longer sounds like an appealing influencer, right? It sounds pretty painful, and that's because it is the major cause of most of our pain.

Many of us have learned to mislabel our judgment as discernment — but there is an enormous difference between the two. When a situation occurs, we have a choice — we can judge or discern. Judgment reacts with big and negative emotions. Discernment sees the issue at hand and gets curious about solutions. It's calm, clear, and laser-focused. Discernment does not deny the problem exists, nor is it some Pollyanna attitude.

Discernment seeks to understand, clarify, listen, explore, and then create innovative solutions to the problem at hand. It's more of a growth mindset that sees the abundance of possibilities and wants to explore them.

The inner critic acts in three distinct ways — it judges yourself, others, and your circumstances. It is trying to keep you safe, but in reality, it is sabotaging you. All of us have this invisible influencer or inner critic. It is part of what some call the flesh. It is the main saboteur draining your confidence and energy, undermining your leadership and your happiness.

Many of us have become so accustomed to this inner critic that it feels like a normal part of us. We trust this voice as the voice of truth — but it is not! When we believe it is the voice of truth, we don't question when the inner critic or any other saboteur comes out in full force in our head. The inner critic's voice either paralyzes you or drives you to work your fingers to the bone — claiming credit for any success — but this is a lie. There is little need for the inner critic.

This inner critic delights in shining a light on all your weaknesses, faults, perceptions, beliefs, thoughts, and feelings. It replays highlight reels of every mistake you have made and quickly compares you to someone it perceives as better than you. It shakes your confidence, and, over time, you shrink away instead of standing up and being heard. This is the voice that keeps you playing small and keeps you from trusting your decisions. It's the voice that has you reach out to 20 people to "get their opinion" before you move forward with a decision. It then recruits your other saboteurs to help reinforce its opinion. Please note that it is just an opinion, or as Stacey Boehman says, "It's just a sentence" (n.d.). Not all opinions are valid and need to be taken on as part of you. The bottom line is that this voice masquerades as a friend, and holds you back from accomplishing your dreams. Notice how the inner critic brings unhappiness, and we all have an inner critic that influences us when we choose the fear pathways of the brain.

This annoying and unhelpful voice makes itself known daily. For some people, it is as loud as a foghorn, making it inescapable. It grates on our nerves like fingernails on a chalkboard. Others have learned to turn the volume down on this voice and not give it as much attention as it wants.

What I'd like you to know is that the inner critic is not helping you, it is hurting you. It is creating distance in your relationships. "The [J]udge pushes you into action through threats, fear, shame, and guilt" (Chamine, 2012, p. 60). But you get to take charge of which voice you listen to and thus which pathway the energy travels.

Just as the Judge is the gang leader for the other saboteurs, the Sage leads other inner voices that come from a place of empathy, curiosity, and creativity — from the thrive region (Chamine, 2012). The Sage pulls you into action through anticipation of the joy of exploration and discovery. This inner wisdom taps into the human desire to find meaning in life and to matter. Your brain desires to make sense of things. All the creative aspects of joy, possibility, and connection happen in this area of the brain. Humans long to connect, care, and belong. This inner wisdom is where we appreciate the mystery of life and move toward our desired outcomes (Chamine, 2012).

The inner critic pushes and has you judging yourself, others, and your circumstances in a negative light. Your inner wisdom pulls by being positive, realistic, and growth-oriented.

As a young girl, the inner critic ruled my mind. This condemning voice broadcast the message I received as a child through my paternal grandparents. The unspoken message was unmistakable: Boys were more valuable than girls. Favoritism was rampant, and Christmas shone the spotlight on that favoritism at their house. My sister and I each received a card with a $5 bill, and the boys received many thoughtful gifts. There is no explaining that to a six-year-old; the message was loud and clear. I remember feeling anger and shame and not wanting to go see them. My resistance to seeing them started a chain reaction of guilt, shame, and anxiety because of my dad's reaction to the resistance.

My parents became parents at 19 years old and did the best 19-year-olds could do to love and care for us. Since the average brain does not fully develop until around age 26, my parents' brains were still developing. I don't recall being able to express emotions without the message of "suck it up, buttercup" being their reaction. It was challenging for a sensitive kid like me. For decades I received the lies that this invisible influencer told me. This intruder told me my sensitivity and gender were defective. This battle in my inner world would continue for more than 40 years. This was the birth of many of my invisible influencers and my drive to be seen, heard, and understood. Add several other childhood traumas to this story, and you can see how these saboteurs develop their power.

I'd like to acknowledge that none of us is exempt from our own parenting regrets. Many of us parented from a place of immaturity and/or fear. The good news is that we don't have to continue to live in this space. We get to move into the power of accessing a different region of the brain.

Every inner critic comes equipped with accomplice saboteurs it recruits to survive difficult things. These invisible influencers worked with my inner critic to get my basic needs met. Every human has the basic needs to be safe, seen, soothed, and secure (Siegel & Bryson, 2021). If we are not choosing how those needs are met, our go-to saboteurs will get the job done in the survive region.

These reactions develop in childhood and then get exercised for decades, gaining strength. And they do work — until they don't. We think they are necessary for our success because they have served a purpose in our lives; but as adults, we no longer need them to survive. These invisible influencers have become our stress patterns of behavior. More about these in the coming chapters.

### Withness Nugget:

The Judge equals condemnation, blame, and shame, all of which are the fruit of the enemy of our soul. Honestly, judgmental and condemning people/pharisees were those who received the harshest words spoken by Jesus. He ate with, called forward, and sat with many sinners, loving them exactly where they were and calling them to more than their present from a place of unconditional love. Yes, he loved us while we were yet sinners (Romans 5:8) AND yet He wants us to choose more. Each of us gets to choose whom we say He is (Matthew 16:15); yet if we choose differently at this time, He still "looks at us and love[s] us" (Mark 10:21) as we stubbornly resist that love.

When we choose to live in that unconditional love with Him, there is peace, confidence, courage, and clarity. We get to rest and quit resisting. We get to connect with others and affect them. We get to live from a place of peace as we abide in love — Jesus Christ. In this space, we accept others as they are, we accept our circumstances, and we can expand into this great love. We accept that we cannot change others and that judging them serves no purpose toward love. We accept what we cannot control and trust in the One who controls it all. We look for gifts, opportunities, and blessings in disguise. We stop judging harshly and instead, accept and discern the next best wise step toward love. Acceptance leads to expansion and abundance. Resistance leads to scarcity, judgment, and shame.

### Mindful Moments:

When you hear the inner critic blasting over the inner radio waves, turn down the volume. Feel your feet on the floor or put them in the grass. Take some slow, deep belly breaths. Inhale through your nose for a count of four, then and hold it for a count of four. Next, exhale through your nose for a count of six. Repeat this at least three times. Using heart-focused breathing can create coherence. Place your hand on your heart and imagine the oxygen entering your heart and exiting your heart. Notice how this affects your heart rate. Notice the depth of your breathing. Now imagine yourself getting curious about that inner critic. How can you have empathy for how that inner critic is just trying to keep you safe? What if you saw this situation as your body's beautiful yet maladaptive defense mechanism just functioning automatically? What if that part of you could step aside and just breathe and relax for a moment?

# Transform Your Brain

 **Journal Your Reflections:**

After your mindful moment, ask the following four questions from Bryon Katie, which she calls "The Work"

- Is it true?

- Can you absolutely know that it is true?

- How do you react, and what happens when you believe that thought?

- Who would you be without that thought?

CHAPTER 9

# THE SABOTEURS WORKING BEHIND THE SCENES

———◆———

Invisible influencers, or as Chamine calls them, saboteurs, jump into action whenever they sense a threat (2012). These threats can develop when there is an unmet need or an uncomfortable, unprocessed emotion. These 10 invisible influencers will take over by default if a stressor is not managed from the thrive region of the brain. Before we begin with an overview, I'd like you to know that we can intercept these patterns. These patterns of behavior do not have eternal control over our lives. This is the work we must do, and the first step is awareness of who these invisible influencers are.

Spotting these invisible influencers is important because we are blind to the things that feel normal to us. In coaching, we call them blind spots. They feel comfortable to us. They are our cruise-control reactions to perceived threats or felt needs. These influencers always join forces with your inner critic, who is the chief saboteur in the survive region, and they all function based on lies.

Each one has a lie that motivates its appearance, and each one believes it is necessary for survival. They actually did serve a purpose, but they don't have to be in charge anymore. Although these influencers may have helped you in the past, it came at a cost — your joy, peace, authentic connection, and deep relationships, to name a few. The more you intentionally look for and see why you need a specific influencer, the more you will see how it is ruling your life. And the good news is, there is a better way to reach your goals, without depending on old tools to get things done.

A universal truth exists in our brains. When we try to resist or avoid something, our brains automatically guide us there instead. The brain will always find what it's looking for. Think about the golf ball in the water. Focusing on avoiding the water hazard was still focusing on the water, so that's where the ball ended up![3]

These invisible influencers are our cruise control. We developed them to protect ourselves physically and/or emotionally in childhood. Although we don't need them in adulthood, many of us don't know how to live without them.

---

[3] *The purpose of this book is not to dive deep in this area, but to bring attention to your brain's patterns. These patterns keep you in survival mode. The "Positive Intelligence" framework (2012), calls on the Enneagram personality model, and like any personality assessment can create biases that stagnate growth. Assessments that do not include real feedback from other humans run the risk of confirmation bias by reinforcing your own view of self. I prefer to see them as patterns of behavior to spur self-awareness, which is the first step to transformation.

The number one influencer is the inner critic. We've already talked about how the inner critic is always associated with negative emotions. This critic leads the pack to send us into an overthinking spin cycle. The inner critic amplifies any insecurity! You can suspect this critic is at work when you feel unhappy.

This inner critic usually recruits two other characters to help you get your needs met. The critic hates to work alone! Your brain will go to the stress patterns you are most familiar with. The wider the road, the easier it is to travel. These recruits keep you playing safe, small and dislike change.

The Avoider hates conflict and often downplays the importance of genuine problems. It procrastinates and avoids until the last possible minute things it perceives as difficult, yet it has difficulty saying "no" because it doesn't want to rock the boat.

The Controller experiences anxiety and impatience to get things done its way. It's the Controller's way or the highway. It is super-competitive and often becomes angry when people do not step in line.

Hyper-achiever is performance-based and focused on all things external. It gives little time to the inner world or emotions, often blocking them out. It seeks to impress others by shape-shifting. Performance equates to worth in its eyes.

Hyper-rational is all about "just the facts, ma'am." We can see it as distant and aloof. Feelings carry no weight in the conversation — they are irrelevant to Hyper-rational. Data rules over people. It underutilizes the relational circuitry in the brain and overutilizes the analytic circuitry.

Hypervigilant is always looking for lions, tigers, and bears. It sees all that can go wrong and rarely sees what is right. When Hypervigilant is supporting the inner critic, anxiety is common, because all it sees is danger everywhere.

The People-Pleaser sees everyone's needs and jumps into action to help them. It helps so much that it loses sight of your own needs, always putting self last. It needs to be liked and tends to over-commit, only to feel resentment later.

The Restless influencer needs activity and excitement. It is busy and has difficulty experiencing contentment in any situation, instead always searching for the missing link in its life or the next fun thing it can do. FOMO rules it. This constant high-energy state keeps it from living in the present.

The Stickler is a perfectionist. It needs everything organized and becomes irritable and critical when there is disorder. It is often black and white in its thinking, lacking any flexibility.

The Victim is a martyr. Ruled by big, negative emotions, it feels misunderstood and alone. Comparison is one of its go-to activities. It often aspires to be rescued by others. The Victim sends off "neediness" vibes.

What I'd like you to notice is that all these invisible influencers have lies and beliefs attached to them. You no longer need to rely on these tactics to get your needs met. Fear and threats fuel invisible influencers.

You can intercept these influencers and act like yourself. The best way to intercept these patterns is to notice their presence in your life. They drive your actions and conversations. Notice this today. Notice how they are associated with negative emotions. When they show up, label them. Siegel and Bryson say we need to "name it [to] tame it" (Siegel & Bryson, 2012, p. 27).

Just bringing attention to your invisible influencers weakens their power over you. They thrive on remaining invisible and maintaining control. When you acknowledge them and thank them, they usually loosen their powerful grip over your decisions.

 **Withness Nugget:**

We no longer need to resort to the ways of the flesh to solve our problems. Although this is a learned pattern of behavior, God has more for you. We get to put off these cruise-control survival techniques. By practicing the pause, we get to choose our pathway as we notice the space between the stimuli and the response. When we shift to the thrive region of the brain, we are putting off our old self and putting on the new self, which is fueled by love and produces the fruit of the Spirit. When we shift to the thrive region of the brain, we get to abide instead of survive. We can tap into the power and abundant life that was meant for us.

"You were taught, with regard to your former way of life, to put off your old self, which is being corrupted by its deceitful desires; to be made new in the attitude of your minds; and to put on the new self, created to be like God in true righteousness and holiness" (Ephesians 4:22-23).

**Mindful Moments:**

When you notice the energy of the same old patterns of thoughts and behaviors welling up, pause and breathe. Notice the energy you are feeling in your body. How does this energy manifest itself? Which body part is calling for your attention? Gently rub two fingers together with such tension that you can notice all the ridges and sensations. Focus on the sensations you are experiencing at your fingertips. The act of noticing these sensations will help guide you to the thrive region of your brain, where you can start acting like yourself again. In this region, you can tap into superpowers that will guide you toward connecting with yourself, others, and God.

 **Journal Your Reflections:**

- Which saboteur most resembles your pattern of cruise-control behavior?

- What need might you be trying to meet as you access that old pattern?

- Is there a situation or circumstance from your past that reminds you of this?

- What is your next best step to live in the present?

- What patterns are you noticing? Reflect on your body and record any new sensations you notice, putting descriptive words on paper. Where in your body do you notice this sensation? Is there tension or weightlessness? Temperature changes? Is there a feeling or numbness? Notice your patterns from a place of curiosity — no judgment allowed.

## Invisible Influencers

"The Avoider" hates conflict and often downplays the importance of genuine problems. They will procrastinate and avoid things they perceive as difficult until the last possible minute. They have difficulty saying no because they don't want to rock the boat.

"The Controller" experiences anxiety and impatience to get things done, their way. It's their way or the highway. They are super competitive and often become angry when people do not step in line.

"The Hyper-achiever" is performance-based and focused on all the external things. They give little time to their inner world or emotions, often blocking them out. Hyper-achievers seek to impress others by shapeshifting. They equate their worth with their performance. These are your workaholics.

"The Hyperrational" is all about "just the facts, ma'am." The hyperrational can be distant and aloof. Feelings are irrelevant to them. Analyzing the data takes precedence over the people involved. They rarely use their relational circuitry.

"The Hypervigilant" is always looking for lions, tigers and bears. They see all that can go wrong and rarely see what is right. Anxiety is their dominant emotion because all they need is danger everywhere.

"The People Pleaser" is the one who sees everyone's needs and jumps into action to help them. They help so much that they lose sight of themselves, putting themselves aside for everyone else. They strongly need to be liked and tend to over-commit only to feel resentment later.

"The Restless" needs activity and excitement. They are busy and rarely experience contentment in their situation. Searching for the next that will make them feel whole. FOMO rules for them. This constant anxiety to do more keeps them from living in the present.

"The Stickler" is your perfectionist! They need everything organized meticulously and become irritable and critical when there is disorder. They are often black-and-white in their thinking and lack flexibility.

"The Victim" is your martyr. Think big, negative emotions! Feeling alone and misunderstood often, we can see them as needy. They often compare themselves to others. They often want to be rescued by others."(Chamine, Positive Intelligence.pg)

CHAPTER 10

# CHANGE THE CHANNEL

———◆———

Before we move on, I'd like to discuss how energy enters from the outside world and is processed in the brain. When information from the outside world enters your system, it gets interpreted through two distinct channels. These channels broadcast information like a radio station. They are called the "data channel" and the "PQ® channel," according to Chamine (2012, p.132-134).

Your data channel transmits words and data (especially numbers and statistics). The "PQ® channel transmits your "energy, your attitude, your emotion and [your] tone" (Chamine, 2012, p.132-134). For our purposes, I will refer to the PQ® channel as the thrive channel. As human beings, we are more influenced by the information that is transmitted through the thrive channel than the data channel (the survive channel). The thrive channel works to either connect or repel. Through the thrive channel, we discern if the energy, attitude, emotion, and tone match the information in the data channel. Through the data channel, we judge and evaluate from a negative viewpoint. Whatever is broadcast through the thrive channel holds more weight in your brain.

Your rational mind loves to tune in to the data channel — its favorite station. Your relational mind tunes into the thrive channel as its favorite station. The thrive channel is also known as your relational circuitry. The relational circuitry allows us to connect with others and be present in the moment. It allows us to keep our identity and the big picture in sight and create new possibilities. Just like the map of the USA, many pathways in our brains intersect as we access this sweet spot.

Richard Boyatzis et al. (2019) would describe this region as the PEA (Positive Emotional Attractors) network. When we access this part of the brain, we can dream, explore, and creatively connect to positive emotions and possibilities. Much of this research has been and continues to be confirmed through fMRI studies of the brain. US-based Amen Clinics has the world's largest database of brain scans and fMRI data. We can thank Dr. Daniel Amen for equipping the scientific community with access to that data. The interpersonal neurobiology, neuroscience, and performance science fields are exploding since applying the fMRI data. We live in an exciting time for neuroscience research.

Where your brain places its attention will affect your perceptions, thoughts, and emotions. The lenses through which we see the world interpret the information. As you notice, looking through the lens of the thrive region is where all the good stuff happens, as we connect with other people. This is where we get to tap into the withness principle of mutual mind and connectedness.

The PQ® channel fuels connection with other humans through empathy, love, joy, peace, patience, kindness, goodness, faithfulness, gentleness, and self-control. It orients our brain in the "toward" direction. We can build our brain muscles to choose this channel (Chamine, 2012).

The data channel runs on fear, or the "away" reaction, in the brain. Its focus is the works of the flesh and performance-based activities. This channel is where we often experience regrets and do things we really don't want to do (Romans 7:15-20). It is an automatic and subconscious pathway. When operating here, we feel disconnected from ourselves, others, and God. I think this quote from Lysa TerKeurst summarizes what we feel like when we are living from the data channel of our brain: "There's a disconnect somewhere between the faith I want and the one I'm living. I know you feel it too. I've seen it in your tear-filled eyes, and I've heard it in your questions about the things hardest to understand about God" (2019, para. 11). The full life of abundance is about closing this gap between knowledge and experience.

Feeling disconnected from God, ourselves, and others is not the way it was meant to be! He made you to connect and affect! You can connect with God, others, and yourself by changing the channel in your brain.

It's good news that we can slow down, pause, and intentionally shift to the thrive channel and change our perspective. As Viktor Frankl says, "Between stimulus and response there is a space. In that space is our power to choose our response. In our response lies our growth and our freedom". In this space we experience a holy-noticing moment (Stone, 2019), in which we can choose to abide or go renegade. This is an intentional process: We get to cooperate and live a full and meaningful life — or not. One of my mentors, Cheryl Scanlan, would remind us that this is the place that we incorporate the 7 Step Shift®. The 7 Step Shift® is a tool used by Promised Land Living Ministries*, Way of Life Coaching, to walk Christ followers to the place of abiding daily and shifting away from survival mode.

The first glimpse of that shift happened for me one painful day. This day was the initial catalyst for change. We've all been there — a specific point in time where we say, "Enough is enough!" This was my moment! I remember the day like it was yesterday!

They came home from school, said hi, then quickly walked right past me to their room.

My blood was boiling, and it was about to overflow!

I had been waiting for them to come home from school all day to discuss the things they left incomplete. They were VERY IMPORTANT THINGS (according to my inner critic).[4]

They didn't even give me the chance to speak to them! My pride reared its ugly head like a groundhog on February 2.

As I thought about it and looked around the house, my fury escalated. So I did what any unseen, unheard, and misunderstood mom would do. I knocked on their door and

---

[4] *https://promisedlandliving.com

walked into their room to "share my heart" with them (aka flip my lid).

After my tirade, the kid who usually showed no emotion turned to me in tears.

I felt the blood leave my face.

I felt my stomach sink.

With a pierced heart, I stood speechless and full of shame!

I remember them saying, "I come to my room to get away from you! I can't stand it anymore! Every time you see me, you nag me to do something! Mom, I can't even breathe!"

At that moment, my world was shredded to pieces. They were right! It was allowing my self-sabotaging and judging thoughts control that sent me on the rampage. My feelings of anxiety, in the moment, drove my words and actions. This low-level hum of anxiety was sucking the life out of my relationship with my children.

I did not behave like myself. (Wilder & Woolridge, 2022)

I saw it differently now — from their perspective. It was as if my kids had no safe place to come to recharge and rest because of MY underlying stress patterns.

I thought, "My kids are getting ready to leave for college in the next few years, and I don't want to have regrets. I don't want to drive them away; I want to influence my kids positively. The dirty socks are not a legacy that I want to leave. I have to figure this out!"

Thanks to my kid's response, I experienced regret, and that was what I needed to make me aware of my need to change.

Retrospectively, I was operating out of my invisible influencers — it was totally fear-based, with tons of charged, negative emotions. The data channel was my main mode of operation; my thrive channel was offline.

I would venture to say, most of our regrets come from the data channel.

When I was functioning from the data channel, I was in "enemy mode" (Wilder & Woolridge, 2022), and anyone in my way was the enemy. Survival mode is where all the overthinking happens. Your brain goes into overdrive to defend, argue, shame, blame, and prove yourself right. No good comes from enemy mode. We must live differently. We must tune in to the thrive channel — the relational circuitry — so we can connect and affect others. We must remap our brains!

### Withness Nugget:

When you live on cruise control, you live with regret. You often do the things you don't want to do. In order to choose to respond instead of react, you need to be willing to get comfortable with being uncomfortable. "For what I want to do I do not do, but what I hate I do And if I do what I do not want to do, I agree that the law is good" (Romans 7:15-16, NIV).

Remember, your brain is trying to keep things status quo to keep you safe. When you feel the discomfort of new ways of thinking and behaving, your brain will fight against itself. The Judge and other saboteurs fight for possession of your brain and body. You are no longer slaves to the old ways of doing things. You are a new creation, with new tools, new possibilities, and new power that lead you to an abundant life.

### Mindful Moments:

Notice the energy you are experiencing. Just get curious — without judgment.

Is the energy positive or negative? Where is it located? What does it feel like (heavy, fluttery, stabbing)? Is there a temperature associated with the energy? Does this energy remind you of anything from your past? When have you felt like this before? Can you name the emotion you are experiencing? If the emotion is negative, are you able to self-regulate with breathwork or sensory shifts?

### Journal Your Reflections:

- What is your dominant station: the PQ® channel or the data channel?

- What effect does this channel selection have on your relationships?

- Are you willing to shift from the data channel to the PQ® channel and solve problems from a resourced place?

- What patterns are you noticing? Reflect on your body and record any new sensations you notice, putting descriptive words on paper. Where in your body do you notice this sensation? Is there tension or weightlessness? Temperature changes? Is there a feeling or numbness? Notice your patterns from a place of curiosity — no judgment allowed.

CHAPTER 11

# THE EXPRESS HIGHWAY TO POSSIBILITY

We've explored Route Survive, which is a familiar pathway to most. Now it is time to put on new sunglasses as we exit onto Route Thrive.

As you ride on Route Thrive, the laughter and singing pulsates from the vehicle. You are enjoying the other passengers. It is a joy just being together on this exciting journey. You are honoring the different spins of the music as one passenger goes solo in song. The delightful sound permeates the car. You marvel at the creativity and experience gratitude for this time. It creates pictures in your mind, reminding you of other times when you felt accepted. Goosebumps rise on your arms and tears fill your eyes. You are experiencing emotion. It is a big emotion, but not threatening. There is this inescapable energy of withness. It draws you to it like a moth to a flame.

You want this moment to last forever because there is so much peace here. There is no judgment that your singing voice is a little off key — just appreciation. You wonder what harmonies will be created as the next songs play. The possibilities are endless as someone taps on the back seat, adding percussion. It adds value, and your eyes sparkle. The journey is exciting because you don't know what's going to come next. There's openness to the possibilities and the collective wisdom of the group — and realizing that the possibilities are endless is wondrous. Driving is no longer boring because each person is showing up authentic and contributing — no more hiding or pretending. It is withness as a witness.

It's a witness to the beauty of God's creation and His power in our lives. It's a witness to the amazing creativity and innovation that is available to you as well as the ability to carry it out in real time. Now you are witness to the connection that bonds people together like glue, seeing the big picture and keeping your priorities aligned with your values. Through this withness you can abide and bear much fruit. You have the space to hear the right voice guide you and take action. You are no longer carried away by tension and drama; instead you're securely anchored in the present moment. You notice your invisible influencers are not as loud, and all you see are possibilities. When those influencers rear their ugly heads, you notice them, but they aren't so loud and you easily shift back to a place of joy.

In this space, you are BEING present in the moment, partnering with God and the life you are in now—not looking in the rear view mirror or in your crystal ball—you are partnering with life Himself. God meets you in deep and miraculous ways from the thrive portion of your brain. If we choose the thrive pathway, we get to cooperate with God and His wisdom in us to create together by faith. We can tap into the joy of the Lord, which becomes our strength (Nehemiah 8:10). This joy comes from the thrive region. It is a fruit that identifies perspective; a fruit of deep, meaningful connection with others and God. When we feel safe in relationship with ourselves, others, and God, we are our best selves at our essence, and fear dissipates.

God has wired your brain for joy! Joy is a gift and fruit from God. This is withness: being present with others and facing our challenges together, giving us strength to bounce back from hardship. Wilder (2020) and Warner (2016) describe this joy as a "glad to be with you" experience. If you don't know it yet, God is glad to be with you! From the beginning He said it is not good for us to be alone (Genesis 2:18). He created us in His image for connection. God delights to connect with you and watch you connect in meaningful ways with others. He delights when you connect with the identity that He has planted in your heart. He delights when we live and walk in our essence instead of surviving inauthentically. This is only possible when we operate in the thrive region. You are able to sit with imperfection and actually find joy in it.

If we were to view people's brains via fMRI when they are experiencing connection, you would notice the social engagement system light up like a Christmas tree. This system alerts the brain and body of safety and allows you to let your guard down and BE real. The hormone oxytocin is released and we feel bonded and deeply connected to the other person and our experience – this chemical release also inhibits the sympathetic response in the nervous system – think calm and connected vs. self-protection and defensiveness. This is the sweet spot! Living in this area of our brain, connected to God, self, and others, is the most fertile ground we can cultivate! We can show up fully present, as is, and attach securely to those we are with.

The Bible tells us to renew our mind (Romans 2:12) and take captive our thoughts (2 Corinthians 10:5). Neuroscience is catching up with what God already knew. Your brain is moldable and can adapt and change the pathways it takes. God has given us the ability to think, to feel, and to experience our world with others. Humans are like no other creature!

Let's face it. The human body is amazing! It is complex and interconnected. Each part is separate but linked. Siegel (n.d.) describes integration as a linkage of the different parts working together. Your brain works most efficiently and produces the most joy when you operate from and filter data through the thrive region of your brain.

Let me explain. When a situation comes up and we filter the situation first through the thrive region, we are open to seeing possibilities. We are filtering the problem through positive and loving lenses. We get to choose this as our main filter. We keep our relationships in sight and don't steamroll over others to accomplish our agenda. When we choose this filter, we listen to understand. We ask questions to confirm what we are hearing. Our values and identity guide us when we are solving problems in this region. We show up as our authentic selves.

When we begin our process of problem-solving through the survive region, fear and self-protection leads the way and often holds us back from seeing the big picture and from trying things that are out of our norm because failure looms over us. When we solve problems from the survive region, personal accomplishment of tasks and goals pushes aside relational problem-solving, often leading to more fear, frustration, or failure.

When we have difficulty shifting to the thrive region, it's a symptom of an unused pathway in our brain. Like a long-unused road that has deteriorated over time, these pathways need some serious maintenance — resurfacing and widening — which is totally possible. If you're resorting to your old ways of problem-solving, then you know your thrive pathways need some maintenance.

This is how this pathway problem showed up for me. Growing up, one of my role models got things by weaponizing anger. The tactics were aggressive words and actions, which moved people by fear. I learned that to get things accomplished, wrath gets the job done. I'm not proud of this, but this is how I functioned for most of my life. What I know now is that when I was getting things done, I was offline from the relational circuitry of my brain and functioning from the survive circuitry.

There was a tech project (a nice, quick drive down the highway) at work that was easy-peasy (in the window of tolerance) but would consume large amounts of time, so I hired a team to get it done. For whatever reason, this easy-peasy drive was thwarted by a multi-vehicle crash (threat) closing all lanes! I felt anger rising from my stomach and heat spreading like wildfire through my chest; my neck and head were pulsating with every beat of my heart. Consumed by the percussion of my heartbeat, I went looking for the team to spew forth my anger, roasting them like marshmallows at a campfire. My anger-as-a-weapon stress pattern was rearing its ugly head, and I was very close to pushing people aside for the sake of getting the project done — the old steamroller technique. This familiar reaction through my survive region was the quickest and easiest detour to take to get around the accident. I knew it well because it had always "worked" for me.

The cool part of this story is that this time I noticed it before I exploded! I took a moment and noticed the sensations I was experiencing, and they did not feel good. What I needed in the moment was self-regulation — a different route around the accident. Noticing the stress patterns is the first step toward intercepting them — this noticing was like an exit sign telling me there was another route I could take. This was another experience, like the one with my kids, that propelled me toward change.

So I chose the different road — an abandoned pathway through my thrive region — and did the work to figure out a better way of getting the project accomplished – other possibilities. It required intentionality as I drove tentatively down this unkept road, but the new view (relational equity) was worth it. I got off the familiar Route Survive to take the vaguely known Route Thrive.

The percussion in my head was loud as my invisible influencers and the inner critic were blaring in full force, trying to drown out *the* voice of Truth. Arrows of doubt and fear regarding my decision to abandon Route Survive were flying at me relentlessly, pointing out the potholes and dangers. But here's the thing: *The* voice of Truth speaks in a soft whisper, and, in order to hear it, we need to quiet ourselves. This time I turned up the volume to *the* voice of Truth when I noticed its whisper. I brought my attention to the still, small voice, remembering that "where your attention goes, your energy flows" (Robbins, 2022).

At that moment, I could see the view clearly, experience the positive energy, and respond instead of giving in to the invisible influencers and letting the negative energy control my reaction. From this place, I was able to quiet the anger and ask myself an important question: "What is the best way right now to deal with this problem?" The problem did not go away, but I wasn't reacting to it either. I responded instead, exploring creative solutions with my team and expressing my feelings calmly and as my authentic self from my relational circuitry. I avoided the multi-vehicle crash, navigated an unused route, and guided the team to the next best steps.

This was difficult at first. This road needed to be widened and repaved, but I now knew it was a good route to take. I saw that there was another route to problem resolution, so new connections (offramps) for my anger were being laid in my memory bank (my map). My hippocampus safely stored this memory so I could pull it from the file cabinet when needed. Taking a moment after the big emotion to focus on the win helped reinforce the positive outcome. In fact, for five hours, following a big win, your brain is integrating this progress, especially if we put it to action. When we are integrating our learning, the neurons are very active and connecting to create new neural pathways. Burning this memory into my brain at the time helped me to choose this pathway more quickly the next time I experienced a major "threat." The bottom line is everyone escaped my enemy mode (Wilder & Woolridge, 2022) without emotional injury or relational rupture.

I learned that integrating both regions of my brain could override my stress pattern. Like many of us, I had mastered survival mode; now it was time for me to thrive by tapping into the power of both regions of my brain functioning together.

With the thrive region perspective leading the way, the brain can listen to reason without negative emotions taking over. All good things begin in the thrive region, so this is the second step. After you notice the internal swirling (first step), choose the better route (second step). The sooner you get on Route Thrive, the more power you have to ignore the lies of your invisible influencers. This is where you act like your best self instead of an inauthentic version of self. The exit to Route Thrive is where you take back your power instead of giving it to those influencers.

Let's go back to my tech story and explore what happened when I first realized I was stuck behind the crash. In this traffic standstill, my negative emotions were big and wild. It felt like the wild, wild west! There were no rules — survival was the name of the game.

Now, imagine yourself in this stuck place for a moment. There is no exit you can see, because your brain only brings your attention to what you already know. At this moment, you may experience one of your inhibitory emotions, such as shame, guilt, or anxiety. These are the emotions society has trained us are acceptable. But all these emotions do is blow the situation out of proportion, so we turn to distractors.

Distractors are behaviors we turn to in order to avoid feelings of discomfort or as a habitual defense mechanism. Their goal is to stop the pain.**

So, you have your invisible influencers that come with all their own little stress patterns (e.g., one of the People-pleaser's stress patterns is eggshell walking) whenever you experience discomfort and do not process the associated emotion fully.+ They originate in the survive region and are your default attempt to keep you safe. And you have distractors, which also originate in the survive region and are defenses to stop emotional pain.

For most people, this is where we live, looping from our distractors (screaming, withdrawal, gray area drinking) to our invisible influencers (people pleasing, perfectionism, hyperachiever). This loop exists in your survive region, because the pathways are wide and well-worn. "Any attempt to dictate what thoughts, feelings, and sensations are proper or improper creates a breeding ground for guilt and shame" (Levine, 2008, p. 74). For some of you, guilt, shame, and anxiety are familiar feelings. This is survive region activity, but there is a better way of processing.[5]

Jim Wilder et al. would describe these as BEEPS (behavior, event, experience, person, or substance) and say these things

---

[5] **Dr. Hilary Jacobs Hendel describes what takes place using a tool called the Change Triangle; she calls the invisible influencers "defenses." You can find this in her book, "It's Not Always Depression" (2018).
+Each time you do not process an emotion, it lodges itself in your body. Over time, unprocessed emotions manifest as physical pain or disease because psychological stress and trauma have a measurable effect on the mind and body (check out "The Body Keeps the Score" by Bessel van der Kolk and "The Body Remembers" by Babette Rothschild).

are used to regulate emotion by increasing pleasure or decreasing pain (2013). These are ineffective ways of managing our internal landscape. These ways often manifest through our invisible influencers when our relational circuitry is offline.

God created our attachment center to attach to Him and others in mutually fulfilling relationships. He made us to connect and affect from a place of joy and love (*hesed* and *agape* love). When we have not established a secure attachment as children, our brains turn to substitutes to soothe our emotional or cognitive distress. Our stress patterns become established. It is all about relieving pain or getting pleasure. Once we have established a stress pattern in our brain, our brain does not want to let go of it, so it becomes our go-to way of dealing with any stressors. There are all kinds of defenses that we turn to for relief, but none of them will satisfy long term. Some of them take on a life of their own, like artificial intelligence gone bad. They rule our decisions, our emotions, and our actions.

Distractors and stress patterns are more common for those who have experienced insecure attachment or have unresolved trauma. It's not enough to quit or white-knuckle them out of our lives; we must reopen healthy pathways to the attachment center and begin maintaining them. When we experience a trigger, we must learn new ways of coping instead of resorting to our distractors or allowing our stress patterns to run amuck. As we face our true emotions, we discover how to soothe ourselves from a space of love, connection, and healthy attachment. This helps us step into our power and act like our authentic selves when under stress instead of turning to maladaptive patterns or distractors. As we rediscover our authentic voice, we are empowered to walk in our purpose.

For many of us, we received messages in our childhood about which feelings are acceptable and which feelings are not, and our invisible influencers scream these messages like flashing emergency vehicle lights. These lights show danger to your brain, which causes you to stuff the "unacceptable" feelings instead of experiencing them. What I want you to notice is that these lights are just trying to give you information, but the information is based on lies.

You may have been told things like, "Good girls don't get angry" — the subconscious message being anger is bad and you are a bad person if you express it. Or maybe you heard, "Suck it up, buttercup." This sends the message that if you have any emotion and express it, you are too sensitive and dysfunctional. "Stop crying or I'll give you something to cry about" may have told you that when you experience sadness, those close to you will threaten or shame you. The messages that can provoke a relational disconnect with your loved ones are endless and unique to your upbringing. The bottom line is that your brain adapted distractor techniques in order for you to function and meet your needs for safety and security. Each time you listened to these negative voices — first your loved one(s), then your saboteurs — you lost a little more of your true, authentic self and the courage to step into your power. Whenever we listen to these voices, we choose Route Survive.

A light was shining on one of my distractors during a medical challenge in our family. For decades, I had an on again, off again relationship with alcohol. It served a purpose in my life for some time (albeit an unhealthy one), until it obviously didn't. Just like other distractors, it worked for a while to get short-term results, but it was not a long-term or healthy way to deal with daily stressors. For years, I was aware of this pattern. I would indulge on a stressful day, then beat myself up at night for breaking my promise to myself. The voice of my inner critic was relentless, leading to a vicious cycle. My brain looped between shame, guilt, and anxiety and my distractors. My brain desired to keep me safe from experiencing emotions that were "off limits" according to my invisible influencers. The byproduct was an inauthentic life and being disconnected from my best self and from the relationships that were most important to me. I was not a present participant in my life. I was not living the full life as a spirit-filled ambassador. Alcohol was holding me back from being my best self.

A few things I knew: I didn't resonate with alcoholism; it wasn't my particular issue. It was a stress pattern that needed to be disrupted and emotions that needed to be processed. For me it was this "gray area drinking" that was a go-to pattern. Through the help of a friend and group of women, I got to a place where I challenged my relationship with alcohol. And for me, I saw it for what it was: a tremendous waste of time and mental energy. When I looked at the benefits of alcohol in my life, I discovered they were all lies supported by my invisible influencers & the quick dopamine hits of my habit loop. When I really thought about it, I couldn't identify a single good thing — not one benefit — for me when I used alcohol. So the next step was noticing what factors brought up the urge to numb my emotions, and this led me to decide to choose different pathways in my brain.

Approaching the problem from the relational circuitry was the key to disrupting this pattern. From here, I could experience my emotions; process them; and make clear, calm, and laser-focused decisions on my next best step. This differed from the cruise-control reactions I'd been relying on. The remapping project was working! When I could connect with others on my journey in a safe, nonjudgmental environment and apply my neuroscience work, a whole new world opened up for me. I was clearing and repaving untraveled pathways instead of repeatedly taking the same ineffective routes. The important work of the group of women I had joined involved relationships, which tapped into the relational circuitry and enabled me to change the pattern. There was support instead of doing it on my own. Having connection with others who are traveling the same journey made all the difference. This is the reason most of the work I do with clients is in a group setting. Transformation happens when we are in relationship with others in a safe, nonjudgmental space, where we can question our thinking and actions. In this space, we get to discuss, challenge, learn new skills, and redefine our relationship with our invisible influencers and distractors.

Rewiring brain pathways is like going to the gym. Having a gym membership does not give you your dream body any more than thinking about mental fitness gives you a transformed mind. It requires reps – these reps help you pave dormant pathways to the thrive region of your brain and strengthen the mental muscles needed to overcome survival mode. This is why I created the Micro-Shift Reset System.® I noticed the challenges professionals faced on the job to put in the reps, so I developed a system of micro-learning, implementation, and gamification as a means of building in these reps in real time without any disruption in your workflow. The reps along with other tools were available for me at any time I left the window of tolerance in my brain. The Micro-Shift Reset System® is my entry level system for on-the-job energy reset.

Any time you feel a big, charged emotion or dysregulated, you can shift your brain to the thrive circuitry and process your experience through the lens of possibility. It requires intentional practice. Just like going to the gym at first includes discomfort, so does brain rewiring. We no longer need to travel on the well-worn but ineffective pathways; now we can choose to repair and maintain once abandoned pathways and turn them into superhighways. You have a choice, just like Viktor Frankl noticed, "between the stimulus and the response there is a space. In that space is the power to choose our response. In our response lies our growth and freedom." What will you choose today?

 **Withness Nugget:**

The flesh and the Spirit battle for your attention. This is an internal battle, a war raging within (Ephesians 6:12) that shows up in real life, as I stated above. These battles are hidden in the church because there are just some things that don't get talked about there. We must change this! Jesus condemned the pharisees who hid their sin and pretended to have it all together — He actually called them whitewashed tombs (Matthew 23:27). We were made to be with, support, and love one another through thick and thin. The real church of transformed believers does not function from a place of judgment and condemnation — this is a survival reaction. This survival reaction is an adaptation to keep our status quo intact, with all our "shiny, happy people."

Jesus calls us to live an abundant life, which can only be accessed when we abandon the survival tactics we developed in our childhood and begin to tap into the thrive region of the brain. It is here we see things like Christ sees them — not with judgment and hate but with love, acceptance, and compassion. It is here that we love and "eat with" sinners just like us! It is here that we meet people at the well, just like Jesus did (John 4:5-30). It is at the well that one can taste and see that He is good (Psalm 34:8). This is what sets us apart; hatred and judgment can't do that because the world already has plenty of those. As we remember the SCARF model of threat and reward responses, we can notice how God wired our brains to respond to His love and the love of His people. Only when the church can show up with love will there be a difference made in our society; this will be the difference that changes everything.

 **Mindful Moments:**

This mindful moment comes from Deb Dana's work (2021) and is an exploration exercise called "Just Like Me." The purpose of this exercise is to move us from a sense of "me" to a sense of "we" by using statements that recognize our similarities, not our differences. Siegel (2023) refers to the way we are "Intraconnected" as "MWe" (Me + We) in his work that explores the integration of self, identity, and belonging.

Here's the exercise credited to Dana. "The autonomic nervous system is the common denominator of all human experience. It allows us to see others as we see ourselves. Our capacity for compassion is grounded in our capacity to be in a ventral vagal regulation" (Dana, 2021, p 144). This exercise helps us see "how other autonomic nervous systems are ordered, organized and activated, just like me" (Dana, 2021, p 142-143). Read the following statements twice — the first time as you think of a friend, and the second time as you think of someone who is not your friend. As you read them, imagine the person in your mind's eye. What state do you notice, are they hyperaroused? Anxious? Angry? What stories are coming up for you? What judgments might you be making about their state?

Just like me, this person experiences times of connection and times of protection.

Just like me, this person responds to cues of safety and cues of danger.

Just like me, this person can disconnect and disappear.

Just like me, this person can feel dangerous.

Just like me, this person can be warm and welcoming.

 **Journal Your Reflections:**

- What counterfeits are your go-to stress patterns, and how can you disrupt them?

- What steps can you take to manage the discomfort that comes from turning to distractors?

- What emotions are hard for you to interact with that drive those distractors?

- How can you demonstrate love for a fellow human and yourself and recognize they are "just like me"?

- What patterns are you noticing? Reflect on your body and record any new sensations you notice, putting descriptive words on paper. Where in your body do you notice this sensation? Is there tension or weightlessness? Temperature changes? Is there a feeling or numbness? Notice your patterns from a place of curiosity — no judgment allowed.

CHAPTER 12

# EMOTIONAL ATTUNEMENT

Tuning in!!! In the neuroscience world, it's called attunement. Attunement, as defined by Merriam-Webster (2023), is "1: to bring into harmony, or 2: to make aware or responsive." WOWZA! Emotional attunement takes more than looking at someone or hearing their words. It means using all our senses to understand what they're feeling and feeling it too. It takes being able to sense, interpret, and respond to someone so that she/he doesn't feel alone any longer. It's a nonverbal bond. When I think about tuning into something, it reminds me of a radio station. Yes, I'm old! In the old days, we would have radios with dials, and you needed to adjust the knob carefully to remove the static and hear the station.

When we tune in to our loved ones, we need to remove the static of distraction, discomfort with emotions, trying to fix others, and all our numbing techniques (social media, Netflix, shopping, drugs, alcohol, gambling, video gaming ... anything that keeps us mindless).

Part of tuning our ears to our loved ones is letting them know they are not alone, so that they feel seen, heard, and understood. It is part of what makes us feel secure enough to form integrated (working) brains.

Many of us are parenting our children just like our parents raised us, and for many of us emotions are really difficult. A significant contributor to this is the fact emotional intelligence was not a thing for our parents. Emotions can be confusing when those responsible for a child's emotional development are emotionally stunted themselves. The result is those lacking emotional maturity often resort to numbing them, pushing them down, and sweeping them under the carpet. We distract ourselves from them at all costs.

Emotions are how we create meaning and intimacy in our life. When someone is experiencing an emotion, you can presume something meaningful is happening for them that is evoking the emotion. Emotions are often motivators (Siegel, n.d.). They focus our attention and energize us to take action.

Siegel (n.d.) describes attunement like this: "When we attune with others we allow our own internal state to shift, to come to resonate with the inner world of another. This resonance is at the heart of the important sense of 'feeling felt' that emerges in close relationships. Children need attunement to feel secure and to develop well, and throughout our lives we need attunement to feel close and connected."

I like to look at emotions as a car dashboard lights up, showing that something is happening under the hood. These emotions begin as chemical reactions at a cellular level. These chemical reactions connect themselves with the chemical messages of a thought — I like to call these chemical reactions "breadcrumbs" in the brain because they set off domino effects in our neural pathways. They are like markers in every experience your memory stores. Your emotions are data that connect your body and brain in a two way communication system (highway) that brings data back and forth. Your emotions can be experienced at different intensities. Emotions are the bridge between thought, feeling and action.

God created us with emotions and what God created should not be denied. These emotions are one way our body communicates with our head and they contain wisdom if we mine them for the data they are trying to provide. When an emotion (energy or sensation) happens in our body, our head tries to make sense of the signal our body is sending it. These sensations signal our brains to retrieve data — images, feelings, and thoughts — from our memory. Our brain then attaches this data to the new emotion, which then drives our actions and behaviors. How complex, wonderful, and awe-inspiring God created us!

### Withness Nugget:

Music connects us to God and to others. It taps into the desire planted in our hearts to worship the Lord with gladness (Psalm 100). Music taps into the thrive region of the brain. It helps us connect movement, creativity, harmony, and positive emotions to the words of the songs. Music helps us memorize words more efficiently.

### Mindful Moments:

Music affects your nervous system. Music can boost your cognitive ability, bring focus, and reduce stress. Notice different styles of music and how they affect you. Notice where in your body you notice this connection. What sensations are connected to the music? Notice the subtleties of the instruments and how they are separate yet linked.

Make a playlist of music that can serve as a resource when you're feeling stressed. Choose songs that bring calm, connection, and joy. Notice if these musical pieces bring rest, energy, restoration, the desire to move, or focus. Perhaps you can sort music based on its physical and emotional effects on your body and mind.

### Journal Your Reflections:

- How has music impacted your nervous system?

- In what ways has music contributed to a state of calm and focus for you?

- Notice what kind of music affects you viscerally. What is it about that music that moves you to emotion?

- In what ways can you use music to self-regulate and improve your performance?

- How can music nourish your soul?

CHAPTER 13

# THE PERFECT FLOW OF TRAFFIC

---◆---

The energy that flows through your body and to your brain contains valuable information for you to explore. This energy starts a chemical change in your body that activates your survive region. Sadly, most people try to silence that energy due to discomfort. What I'd like you to notice is that the emotions you experience have a short life span. Experiencing that energy is like riding a wave. It has a beginning, a middle, and an end. Some waves are bigger than others and last a little longer. The waves, just like the waves in New Jersey, are short-lived. These waves of emotion last for 60-90 seconds (Taylor, 2008).

When a wave comes, we can pause and choose our pathway. The fear pathway will amplify the emotion and create a tsunami. When we choose the fear pathway, it's like trying to hold the ocean back with a surfboard. It's impossible. Those emotions build internally when we choose to ignore them and stuff them down to the depths — they fester. I'd like you to know buried emotions always come back to life. They come back at the most inopportune times and shape-shift into volcanic eruptions. When we push our emotions down by numbing or stuffing, they lodge themselves in our body, causing aches, pains, and disease (van der Kolk, 2015; Rothschild, 2000). The cruise-control reaction desires to stop the negative emotion STAT! This is when all our distractors and invisible influencers come to the scene. You know this too well — it's your go-to pattern of resolving emotions. Surviving trauma trains these patterns. They were helpful at one point, but they no longer serve you.

Experiencing an emotion through the relational circuitry allows you to acknowledge it, feel it through to completion, and then tap into the thrive region to discern your next best step. Fully acknowledging and experiencing what is truly happening results in you showing up as your best self. My best self doesn't just think ABOUT what Jesus would do. Thinking about Jesus takes us through the analytical side of the brain, which is devoid of relational pathways — think performance-based religion. My best self thinks WITH Jesus from love and mutual mind connection (Wilder, 2020).

Before the crowd boos, let me clarify. We want to use our entire brain when interacting with God and others because only then will love be our guiding motive. Remember the vine and branches? It's impossible to bear fruit without being connected to the vine. Being integrated and activating all of your brain with intention is when your best self shows up. You are fully engaged and connected with self, others, and God. This is where your joy and peace lie. It is an internal space of withness adds depth to life and relationships.

Do not fear this energy flow. This is a normal part of life. Energy flows in and out of your body. This energy is a messenger. It sends data for you to notice. This is the first step to choosing your pathway.

The brain and body work together to leave mile markers along the pathways. Each pathway has its own unique mile markers — tastes, sounds, smells, touches, and visual pictures, and there are memories attached to each marker. When one mile marker gets highlighted by sensory input from the brain, it will send you on that familiar pathway. We notice this with traumatic experiences, where these sensory triggers can send you right back in time to the experience of the trauma. According to van der Kolk, "When people relive their trauma, the timekeeping part of the brain that tells you 'that was then' and 'this is now' goes offline" (2019). If you have not experienced trauma, you may have noticed this when hearing an old song and being flooded with memories of high school. These memories are the mile markers on the pathways in your brain.

We can notice how this comes into play with our habits. Clear (2018) and Duhigg (2014) describe how these triggers activate a habit loop in the brain. Mile markers line your neural pathways, just waiting to jump into action. When building new pathways in the brain, we add new mile markers that lead us to the offramp of our choice.

Back to my story from chapter 1. The smell of the pot roast activated a pathway in my brain toward comfort, love, and connection. When I entered the house, it immediately brought me to the relational pathway toward safety. As I traveled deeper into the house, the mile markers of negative experiences created an energy shift, and I abandoned the relational pathway for self-protection and reacting to the threat.

Building new pathways is the deeper work that we do in group and one-on-one coaching. For now, I'd like you to notice what mile markers keep directing your choices. The first step to changing is awareness. This energy that you notice is just data to help you make powerful decisions.

This is exciting work toward maturity and wholeness. Noticing triggers is a gift and opportunity to grow and develop. Each choice we make will either draw us near or push us away from our best selves. With awareness comes growth, and growth should not feel threatening. If you notice yourself feeling threatened, you have returned to the survive region. Notice and reset, with mindful, micro-shifts or by bringing your attention to your breath. You can do these anywhere when you need to reset your brain.

As you tune in, you can add new mile markers that will filter data through love, gratitude, forgiveness, compassion, and all the good things held in this part of the brain. Adding mile markers allows you to reinforce these new pathways and strengthen these brain muscles.

### Withness Nugget:

"Everyone should be quick to listen, slow to speak, and slow to become angry" (James 1:19). "In repentance and rest is your salvation, in quietness and trust is your strength" (Isaiah 30:15).

### Mindful Moments:

Your social engagement system receives its data from your senses through the vagus nerve and delivers the data to the brain. Consider that you were made to connect with other humans. Practice maintaining eye contact with someone. Notice the color around their pupils. Notice their lashes. Really see the other person from the lens of empathy and love. Eye contact with someone you love can release oxytocin, soothing anxiety. You may notice some resistance or discomfort while maintaining eye contact. Don't judge yourself, just get curious about what your brain might be trying to protect you from.

Other ways to increase your social engagement system are singing, laughing, movement like dance or exercise, playing, art, or creativity. Just get curious about what helps you connect with the social engagement system in your brain. Notice which tool(s) you might like to choose regularly to strengthen your relational pathway.

### Journal Your Reflections:

- When you tune in to others, yourself, and God, what are you noticing?

- What are the things you turn to (distractors) when your emotions become uncomfortable (think of the eye contact drill above)?

- What immediate steps can you take to add new and healthy breadcrumbs to your brain's pathways? Will you choose to build these steps into your regular routine?

- What patterns are you noticing? Reflect on your body and record any new sensations you notice, putting descriptive words on paper. Where in your body do you notice this sensation? Is there tension or weightlessness? Temperature changes? Is there a feeling or numbness? Notice your patterns from a place of curiosity — no judgment allowed.

# CHAPTER 14
# MINDFULNESS, MINDSIGHT, AND MUTUAL MIND

When traveling within the window of tolerance, we experience harmony. Leaving the window can lead to chaos (hyperarousal) or rigidity (hypoarousal). We attune to our surroundings when we are in the window of tolerance. There are three unique yet entwined ways we can look at what happens in the inner world of noticing our present moment. The first we will explore is called "mindsight."

Siegel describes mindsight as the ability to see the internal world of self and others, not just to observe behavior — but it involves what you sense and feel. Mindsight enables us to focus our attention from a state of calm, open, clear, receptive and peaceful awareness — when in the window of tolerance — with openness, objectivity, and observation. (Siegel, 2015, p.126-127) It allows us to explore our internal and external stimuli from a perspective of clarity — with mindsight we can shift the focus on the sensations, feelings, thoughts, and images we are experiencing — instead of remaining a victim of our inner world — directing our attention to what's important. (Siegel & Bryson, 2012, p.110) Mindsight creates space to regroup and come back to center. From the center — in the window of tolerance — we can see a situation without distortion, without being swept away or absorbing others' big emotions, and we can decide what would best support the other person and ourselves, in the moment. "Mindsight is the mechanism that allows social and emotional intelligence to occur" (Siegel, 2012). "Insight + empathy = mindsight" (Siegel & Bryson, 2012, p. 121). Mindsight is instrumental in equipping us for healthy relationships.

The second aspect of exploring our inner and outer world is mindfulness. When we are mindful, we are present in the moment — we are intentional and non-judgmental. Mindfulness is about being present externally and internally through a felt sense of experiencing the moment through noticing and self-awareness. It involves the senses and the emotions. Stone refers to Christian mindfulness as the "art of holy noticing — noticing with a holy purpose — God and His handiwork, our relationships, and our inner world of thoughts and feelings" (2019, p. 32). Stone talks about the space between the stimuli and our response as this sacred space of holy noticing (2019).

The third of the three inner states is called mutual mind. This shared mental state is like mindsight and is available to anyone who has a mutual connection with God — the result of this is love. Mutual mind is when you think with God and others instead of about them. This is a communication that can take place without words based on visual cues, voice tone, and the felt sense — it connects us mind-to-mind with another and God. You create a mutual mind when in a mindful state of presence. A mutual mind state refers to the way two people read, connect, and synchronize with each other. Willard (2021) speaks of this mutual mind state with God as His nearness. He is always near you; however, until you tap into the relational circuitry, you will not think and act like Him (Wilder, 2020). God intends for you to connect with and hear from Him.

This mutual mind state of unspoken connection between self, others, and God is what I call withness. "Mutual mind states work by using mirror neurons. These neurons resonate when they see something that resembles their activity in another mind" (Warner & Wilder, 2016, p. 101). "Mirror neurons respond only to an act with intention, where there's some predictability or purpose that can be perceived."(Siegel & Bryson, 2012, p. 124). This mutual mind state links identity, motivation, discipline, activation of potential, vision, and even group identity.

An example of the mutual mind state is when one face lights up in response to another face — it is a happy-to-be-with-you experience. If we focus strictly on the words and are in a highly analytical state when engaging in deep conversation, we do not experience a mutual mind state. Mutual mind is a resonance and understanding with the other person, even if we are not in agreement. But here's the kicker: Your brain allows this mutual mind state only with others who it perceives are like you — in intention, purpose and with some predictability (Siegel & Bryson, 2012, p. 124).

For Christians, we can embody a mutual mind state of nearness to God and others. When we are in a withness state with God or others, we can step more fully into our identity and character — not just notice and observe it, but experience God's presence within it all. This is what I love about group coaching. Clients who are like-minded come together to grow in character as they learn how to step into their authentic self. I've found that when we come together with intention, we experience this witness state.

Many who enter these coaching groups are experiencing this for the very first time.

The brain that has experienced trauma has more difficulty syncing with others on this deep level because of a disruption of their attachment. But there is hope! Even those who have experienced trauma can learn to attune to others and rebuild harmony in their mind. Remember the out-of-tune instrument that Betz describes in the symphony? Those who have experienced trauma quickly notice the out-of-sync internal landscape as their brain alerts them to threats, real or imagined. They quickly leave the window of tolerance and show dysregulated emotions, having difficulty staying "with" the other person.

Spending group time with others who are also moving toward more consistent witness helps a person better learn how to stay attuned. In group, those who have experienced trauma catch glimpses of witness and learn to access new and healthy pathways of connection with others, self, and God. When you are in safe relationships where you can be real, without hiding — where you can show up with your stuff, as is — change happens! Sharing stories in safe spaces breaks chains and eliminates shame. If you've not experienced this kind of safe community, I want you to know that this is where growth really happens! Find a safe place so you can flourish. Groups foster accelerated growth and help you discover your authentic self.

What I'd like you to notice about the place in the brain where mutual mind occurs is that it encompasses identity, attachment, values, remembering and appreciating memories or lessons from the past, emotional regulation/maturity, desires, dreams, and application of moral thoughts. This is the heart of our character. I believe this is where God is telling us to love Him with all our being. We've all felt the piercing and satisfying presence of God whether we realized it or not. God desires us to interact intimately with Him and others — this is withness as a witness. It is an experience of being known, loved, and accepted in your as-is state. Here you are seen as and encouraged to be your "what can be" state.

When we get on Route Thrive, we see the world differently. We get to see things as they can be and explore different perspectives. Life becomes full of possibilities instead of obstacles. When on Route Thrive you experience resilience and a growth mindset. Our ability to innovate allows us to see the big picture. We get to connect with those around us in empathy and compassion. We see things more like Him — through eyes of compassion and love — and we behave more like our authentic selves. These things are available to us and MORE (abundantly more than we can think or imagine (Ephesians 3:20)) when we choose to be relational. When we stay connected, we can be calm, clearheaded, confident, focused, and courageous.

Cling to His promises and commit to His process of fruit production in your life.

We are told by Jesus, "'Love the Lord your God with all your heart and with all your soul and with all your mind.' This is the first and greatest commandment. And the second is like it: 'Love your neighbor as yourself'" (Matthew 22:37-39). This is integration — living whole and living loved — different parts that are linked and work together in harmony. It is here that we experience joy and peace.

 **Withness Nugget:**

Notice what happens for you in this space of withness. Notice what thoughts you have and what emotions come up. Where do you feel energy or tension in your body? Does this energy draw you near to or pull you away from connection with God, others, and your authentic self? This is the discovery process that will help you get real with yourself. Imagine yourself fully connected to God, yourself, and others, grounded and rooted in His love (Ephesians 3:17).

"When our Christianity is only in our conscious mind, our attention shifts from one virtue or sin to another but forgets to monitor the rest of our character; this is slow-track thinking" (Wilder, 2020, p.41). "Character, maturity, and identity are displayed and communicated by the fast-track in the brain. The fast track is where our reactions to circumstances happen quickly, before we can think about them. Your actions reveal your character. The way to change our character and reaction is to think WITH God from the fast track through hesed attachment with God in mutual mind" (Wilder, 2020 p.42). When we do our sensory exercises, we get ourselves to the fast-track area of our brain and build pathways that become superhighways for our fast-track to choose in the future.

**Mindful Moments:**

Imagine yourself in God's presence, totally enveloped in His loving embrace. His eyes of love and compassion pierce your heart as you feel warmth radiate through your body. Your heart is overflowing with love and gratitude as you experience His presence and connect with others in the midst of His presence. Mutual mind experiences with God and others are the abundant life, because we feel safe and secure in His presence. There is no reason to hide because you are complete in Him. You are safe being authentically you — you can rest. "Be still and know that [He is] God" (Psalm 46:10).

 **Journal Your Reflections:**

- Think back to an experience of the nearness of Christ. Describe the sensations you felt in your body. What was this experience like for you?

- How does approaching God from this space of safety and security bring the scripture alive for you?

- What patterns are you noticing? Reflect on your body and record any new sensations you notice, putting descriptive words on paper. Where in your body do you notice this sensation? Is there tension or weightlessness? Temperature changes? Is there a feeling or numbness? Notice your patterns from a place of curiosity — no judgment allowed.

 **Breathe**

The word breath in Hebrew is *ruach*, which means Spirit. When God formed man, He breathed (*ruach*) life into us through His Spirit. The *ruach* of God is with you right now, and as we take an intentional breath, we create space to invite a shift into the intentional presence of God.

Genesis 2:7 says, "Then the Lord God formed a man from the dust of the ground and breathed into his nostrils the breath of life, and the man became a living being."

Breathing affects your brain and your heart and is imperative for nervous system regulation. Deep, intentional breathing activates the parasympathetic nervous system through the vagus nerve so you can rest and digest. The way God designed our bodies is amazing. Breath = Spirit — Spirit leads us to rest. As we breathe deeply, we slow down enough to holy notice the presence of God with us, and we receive His rest.

Matthew 11:28-30 reminds us of where our rest comes from "Come to me, all you who are weary and burdened, and I will give you rest. Take my yoke upon you and learn from me, for I am gentle and humble in heart, and you will find rest for your souls. For my yoke is easy and my burden is light."

What truth will you take away from these thoughts?

## CHAPTER 15

# DANGER AHEAD

---

Emotions are taboo for many secular and religious circles. We avoid them like a plague, and I understand where that fear comes from — it's the desire to manage and control situations. We want things to fit nicely in a man-made theological box so it can all be explained. What I know about God is that He hates boxes! God can do "far more abundantly beyond all that we ask or think, according to the power that works within us" (Ephesians 3:20, ESV). "'For my thoughts are not your thoughts, neither are your ways my ways,' declares the Lord. 'For as the heavens are higher than the earth, so are my ways higher than your ways and my thoughts than your thoughts'" (Isaiah 55:8-9, ESV).

This does not sound like box-living to me. God despises being put in a box of some religious person's imagination of a theological framework that dots all the i's and crosses all the t's. God knows I've been guilty of this Bible-banging, pharisaical behavior. What I notice is that denying or stuffing emotions is really just living on Route Survive. People who suppress their emotions are trying to control their godliness and righteousness or perfectly perform for God. David, speaking to God, said, "You do not delight in sacrifice, or I would bring it; you do not take pleasure in burnt offerings. My sacrifice, O God, is a broken spirit; a broken and contrite heart you, God, will not despise" (Psalm 51:16-17).

When you notice yourself controlling and micromanaging, just know you are not behaving in the full strength of your being and character — your essence, which was made to connect and affect. When we are in control mode, we put problems above relationships, thereby sacrificing relationships for rules.

Warner and Wilder (2016) use the imagery of an elevator as another way to compare and contrast connecting and affecting versus controlling and micromanaging.

In a nutshell, they say that the brain has an express elevator (aka the fast-track system), which has four levels to travel (we won't get into the levels here). This express elevator moves fast, running from level one through level four in approximately one-sixth of a second; given that blink-of-an-eye timing, most of what is happening is without conscious thought. When your fast track works effectively, you are responding from a relational point of view. When your fast-track elevator gets stuck, the problem stops on the fear and task-management floor of the brain — the slow track.

Why is this important? When we travel fully up the fast-track express elevator, our "penthouse executive" is put in charge. If the elevator gets stuck, our "manager" takes control. When the penthouse exec is in charge, we process problems from a relational and joy-filled space, which connects us to higher thinking, unlimited possibilities, our identity and values, and big-picture thinking. There is love, joy, curiosity, appreciation, kindness, and healthy communication. When the manager is in charge, problems are processed with blame, shame, fear, frustration, failure, and disconnection (Warner & Wilder, 2016). We want to reach the penthouse so the executive is in charge.

In the fast track, joy, identity, and mutual mind processing happen (Warner & Wilder, 2012). This is where we can connect with God, others, and ourselves from an authentic place. When your elevator gets stuck, the manager amplifies the problem, making a mountain out of a molehill.

What are the signs that your elevator is stuck and has not reached the penthouse? Dr. Karl Lehman states:

- You don't feel like being around someone you normally like.
- You just want to make a person or problem go away.
- Your mind is locked onto something upsetting.
- You become aggressive in the way you interrogate, judge, or fix people.
- You don't want to make eye contact.
- You feel like it is their fault if they get hurt by something you say or do.

(Warner & Wilder, 2016, p. 129.)

## ATTACHED, INTEGRATED, AND WHOLE

Imagine what life would be like if we always traveled Route Thrive (the fast track) and filtered all that happens through the relational circuitry. You'd find love and joy and be glad to be with others. Those who experienced secure attachment while growing up can access this region more readily.

God said in the beginning that it is not good for man to be alone (Genesis 2:18). We attach to other humans and to God. The Hebrew word for this attachment love is *hesed* (to learn more about this, see Jim Wilder and Marcus Warner's books). We show this secure attachment as we are mindful, have mindsight, and experience mutual mind moments. Many of us live distracted lives, but we were created for more. God has planted the desire for this "more" in our hearts. Every time it feels like something is missing, consider your attachment. Every time the invisible influencers get too loud, remember: "Often what seem to be our deepest desires are really just our loudest desires" (Keller, 2019). What we are learning here is how to shift to meet our deepest desire — we were created by LOVE in order to love and live through love. We were created to connect and affect.

Let me say, I am far from arriving! My work is continuous, and so is yours if you choose to stop living on cruise control. We've made the case that the cruise-control life on Route Survive is unfulfilling! It robs you of joy and peace and keeps you striving for more on the hamster wheel of performance. Route Thrive is a life of relationship, not religion, because religion stems from fear. Abundance flows in the life of love. The life of love is where the possibilities are limitless. It is a life of intention and a life that makes a difference. A life that others are happy to be with is contagious. The more you are living it, the more you aspire to be with others who are living it. Living it shines a light on the emptiness of the distractors. It's a journey toward love and away from fear, and it's a journey worth traveling.

 **Withness Nugget:**

God repeatedly commands us to "fear not." This is very clear. God wants us to live in a place of love, not fear. The Word tells us that "[t]here is no fear in love. But perfect love drives out fear, because fear has to do with punishment. The one who fears is not made perfect in love" (1 John 4:18). God wants us to trust Him with our complete selves, even our emotions. When we fear, we are putting ourselves in the control tower of life. We are trying to direct our lives like an air traffic controller directs air traffic. God desires us to live in withness with Him, others, and ourselves. When we connect with God from the relational circuitry, we get to experience love, joy, and all the fruit of the Spirit as we abide in Him. Our emotions become an avenue of delight, being in the presence of the One who is light. "You make known to me the path of life; in your presence, there is fullness of joy; at your right hand are pleasures forevermore (Psalm 16:11, ESV). "For our heart is glad in Him, because we trust in His holy name" (Psalm 33:21, ESV). "The Lord your God is in your midst, a mighty one who will save; he will rejoice over you with gladness; he will quiet you by his love; he will exult over you with loud singing" (Zephaniah 3:17).

We get to quiet ourselves with God and others when big emotions threaten to rob our joy. Warner and Coursey discuss the concept of interactive quieting in their book, "The 4 Habits of Joy-Filled People." They state, "Interactive quieting refers to activities we do with others that help us to calm our strong emotions and quiet our bodies. It refers to the relational dance that happens when we encounter high-energy emotions. We mirror what people are feeling[,] then we slowly calm down enough to make the feelings more manageable while we stay connected" (Warner, et al, 2023, p.60).

**Mindful Moments:**

Processing emotions takes less than two minutes and is good for your body, soul, and spirit. For the Bible scholars out there, this is not a New-Agey influence — science backs this. There is a brain–body connection.

When I say processing emotions, I mean noticing the energy you are experiencing. Begin with some deep belly breaths. Slow down your breathing and pay attention to the energy. Bring your attention to where this energy begins in your body. What is the temperature of this energy? What is this energy trying to tell you? Is it alerting you to a threat? Is this threat real or imagined? Is the threat true, and can you really be certain that it is true? Who do you become when you react based on assumptions? Is there a trampled boundary or value of yours at work here? Just get curious and don't judge yourself. If the Judge shows up, do a PQ® rep (breath or sensory work) and return to route thrive, where all good things happen. (Continued)

 **Mindful Moments:**

Continued...

This is exploring your inner world and learning to challenge it. Often the Judge comes in to condemn us for feeling an emotion that we learned was off-limits. Remind yourself these are learned patterns and then return your attention to the sensation. Notice when your Inner critic shows up; acknowledge him/her and tell him/her to step aside. Ask yourself questions and notice the gift and opportunity of experiencing this emotion fully. Give it a name — "Oh, this is just sadness; I recognize this emotion." You need to name your emotion for what it is in order to reframe it. Siegel & Bryson say, "Name to tame it or reframe it" (2012, p.27). This reaction is alerting you to the fact that something just occurred with another human being that has been painful.

Get curious. Why has that behavior triggered such emotional pain? Where have you seen this emotion before? What stories are you telling yourself about this emotion? Are they true? Can you just be present with this emotion and ride the wave until completion? Can you remind yourself of your humanity? Are you willing to have compassion for yourself when a sad event triggers an emotion? Soothe yourself like you would a toddler in distress. With a toddler, you would sit with them and just hold them for a minute until it passes. You would be present in their suffering. Sit with yourself — rather than abandoning yourself — and express how you feel. Be present in the moment. You deserve the 60-second break it takes to feel the neurochemical release in your body as you soothe yourself. Once soothed, a toddler gets up to run off to play. You are now ready to reenter relationships with others with compassion for yourself and them. Notice that the others involved are just like toddlers with bottled-up, unprocessed emotions too, "just like me." This is the human experience. Don't judge them — feel compassion for them. You can be this support for yourself and others. Just taking these holy-noticing moments to mindfully connect to your inner world will change everything for you. It will conserve your energy and leave you refreshed.

**Journal Your Reflections:**

- Where have religious beliefs about emotions influenced your inner landscape?

- How can you learn to love your emotions as part of your whole package?

- What would one outside-the-box step be to practice sitting with your emotions?

- What patterns are you noticing? Reflect on your body and record any new sensations you notice, putting descriptive words on paper. Where in your body do you notice this sensation? Is there tension or weightlessness? Temperature changes? Is there a feeling or numbness? Notice your patterns from a place of curiosity — no judgment allowed.

CHAPTER 16

# FROM EMOTIONAL SLAVERY TO EMOTIONAL LIBERATION

---

"Vulnerability is the birthplace of love, belonging, joy, courage, empathy, and creativity. It is the source of hope, empathy, accountability, and authenticity. If we want greater clarity in our purpose or deeper and more meaningful spiritual lives, vulnerability is the path" (Brown, 2015, p. 34).

One of the key lessons that I needed to learn when I started exploring my emotional state was responsibility. For decades I gave up a lot of control of my emotions to sources outside of me. When I discovered I get to choose to be 100% responsible for myself and I get to be 100% responsible to others, many things changed for me.

For most of my life, I took responsibility for things that were not mine to be responsible for. If someone was in a bad mood, it was my fault or job to change this. I empathized deeply with someone who was struggling, as if I were experiencing the crisis myself. If a friend called and asked to talk with me, I immediately thought I did something wrong and a wave of anxiety rolled through my chest.

As a highly empathetic person, I saw this as a good thing and often wondered why people did not reciprocate when they noticed I was upset. I thought it was empathy, when in reality it was porous boundaries. My desire to be loved and connected to others had me placing my focus on everything that was outside of me. This was a huge lesson in my own emotional liberation. When I first practiced my new communication skills, it was rough. There was a clear evolution of growth (Rosenberg, 2015), and I was watching it play out in full color.

What I came to discover is that the way I was receiving stimuli from the outside world was problematic. As we talk about trauma, you will see the root of the problem; but for now, I'd like you to consider where your focus is at this moment. Is it on things outside of you that you cannot control? If so, this section is for you.

The act of being responsible begins when we understand that we always have a choice. We have a choice in how we respond to our circumstances. Remember, when your brain defaults to the tried-and-true pathways, you are deciding based on previous habits, threats/rewards, or interpretations. Your brain will always find what it is looking for; so, if you are looking for how you are a victim in a situation, you will find evidence to prove yourself right. However, if you are determined to see your circumstance from a space of choice and responsibility, you will feel empowered and take full responsibility for your internal landscape. We get to choose the relationship we maintain with our circumstances — and for me, this was so freeing.

In his book "Nonviolent Communication" (2015), Rosenberg talks about hearing negative messages. These negative messages begin a chain reaction of learned perceptions, patterns, thoughts, and emotions. We get to choose how we receive what others say or do. In each moment, our reactions connect to our current needs, expectations, and values.

Rosenberg (2015) discusses four options for us when we hear a negative message. The first option is when we take a negative message personally — hearing only blame and criticism. Internalizing the negative message undermines our confidence and leaves us feeling shame, guilt, and depressed.

The second option is to go on an all-out attack against the other person who delivered the negative message. When we externalize the negative message, we blame the messenger, complaining it's all their fault. Reacting from this survival pattern only throws fuel on the fire — leading to anger for both parties.

The third option is evaluating the data and exploring our inner world. When we ask what our own feelings and needs are, we are curious, and the negative message can be turned into a gift or opportunity. We might acknowledge that their words hurt, but then we self-reflect on why those words hurt us so much (Rosenberg, 2015).

The final option is to remain calm and regulated. When we do this, we can tap into our relational circuitry and get curious about the other person. This curiosity might lead us to empathetically ask questions about the situation and how the speaker viewed it. We might curiously ask, "Are you feeling hurt because you need more consideration of your preferences?" This takes the last level of communication from the inside and turns it toward others with empathy and compassion (Rosenberg, 2015).

What's so brilliant about these options is that Rosenberg shows us that the most effective communication connects your feeling(s) with a need, because underlying every judgment or conflict is an unmet need. Our values and needs are linked. When there is a violation of something we value, we feel internal conflict. This provides an opportunity to self-regulate and get curious about the triggering event. The truth is that "judgments, criticisms, diagnoses, and interpretations of others are all alienated expressions of our own unmet needs" (Rosenberg, 2015, p. 52). Indirect ways of communicating will probably be received as criticism by others, and this brings us back to the five domains of threat and reward in the brain (Rock's SCARF model), throwing the listener back to the survive region by activating a threat response. If we default to our survive region, we get defensive and/or counterattack — we go into enemy mode. The best solution is to respond, creating win-win situations by exploring with nonjudgmental curiosity what each party needs and what they would like to request because of those needs.

We know we have been liberated emotionally when we can take full responsibility for our intentions and actions as we respond with compassion and love instead of fear, guilt, shame, and blame. We have become liberated when we no longer take responsibility for others' emotions, but become responsible to speak to them honestly and from a place of unconditional love and acceptance. Learning to clearly and directly communicate from a place of love, compassion, and empathy is the mark of emotional liberation.

According to Rosenberg (2015), there are three stages on the journey from emotional slavery to emotional liberation. The first stage in emotional slavery is when we take responsibility for everything. In this stage we function in people-pleasing mode, concerning ourselves with things that are none of our business. In slavery, we have no ability to set boundaries with others because we don't know where we begin and someone else ends.

When we move out of emotional slavery and into the next stage, we understand we are not responsible for others' happiness or pain. We have head knowledge of this truth but are not sure yet how to apply it in real life. Our attempts at establishing boundaries might show up in obnoxious or passive-aggressive ways. Personally, when I was learning to self-differentiate and step into my power, people were more like enemies to me.

When we reach the final stage — true emotional liberation — we are 100% responsible for our own intentions and actions AND we are responsible to others. We have learned how to apply boundaries and communicate our needs authentically (Rosenberg, 2015, pp. 57-64).

One last point is that other people's opinions are just feedback. Feedback is neutral; we get to evaluate the validity of feedback through eyes of curiosity and love. The way a person experiences you could be valuable feedback and an opportunity to grow. On the flip side, when there is unresolved conflict, sometimes our view of the other person is tainted, so we see them through the eyes of judgment. Remember, your brain will always find what it is looking for. Becoming self-aware and evaluating feedback from a neutral stance provides us valuable information to assess and potentially grow from. When we learn how to self-regulate, we can step back and observe what is behind the feedback we are receiving. There is freedom and authenticity here. May we run hard after unconditional love and mature communication.

## EMOTIONALLY LIBERATED COMMUNICATION

As we communicate from a place of emotional liberation, we communicate our needs, values, and desires with others in a clear and authentic way. We no longer neglect or ignore our own needs as a badge of honor. Emotionally liberated communication involves win-win conversations, where you are fully present in your circumstances. Emotionally liberated communication happens without hiding or inauthenticity. By engaging the relational circuitry in the brain, one can courageously and kindly speak and be heard.

For the emotionally liberated communicator, there is a balance between what one wants and needs and what others want and need. When we are engaging from the relational circuitry, we are observing, feeling, and aware of our and the other person's needs from a nonjudgmental and curious space. Learning to express our needs from a resourced space increases the likelihood that others will respond compassionately to us.

Demands shut down communication and create a threat scenario in the brain, increasing resistance. This is often the problem for those who are just beginning this journey of healthy, authentic communication. We expect toddlers to respond unfavorably to demands; this is not where adults should be operating. I believe neuroscience and self-regulation hold the key to communicating from an emotionally liberated space.

Having conversations from an emotionally liberated space requires grounding and resourcing yourself — getting yourself to a place of nervous system balance using mindfulness tools. Getting yourself on Route Thrive, where you respond from the relational circuitry, instead of Route Survive and its accompanying fear-based reactions, is step one. Begin by grounding yourself with breathing techniques, micro-shifts or other sensory/mindfulness techniques. Beginning here empowers you to connect with the person in front of you so that you can affect them. It enables you to tap into empathy, curiosity, innovation, and big-picture thinking and then consider the best ways to conduct a win-win conversation and make wise decisions.

When we start from a grounded and resourced space, we notice what we want is the desired outcome of the conversation. Starting anywhere else is the survive region talking! We need to get serious with ourselves: What do I want and need from this conversation? Then we can ask about and consider the other person's wants or needs from this conversation and how we can incorporate both to connect and affect. This type of communication is listening inward, listening outward, and listening under the surface of the words expressed. This communication asks questions first before jumping to conclusions or assumptions. It shines a light on observations and gets curious about one's own interpretation of the observation. Remember, your brain will always find what it's looking for, so get curious about what is fueling it.

How can you communicate in "clear, positive, concrete action language that reveals what we want" (Rosenberg, 2015, p. 70)? This question might best be answered by first stating how we shouldn't communicate. When we communicate in vague language, we are often misunderstood, and then we make assumptions that the other person doesn't care about our needs. Also, if we just express what we feel without including the desired action we are asking/needing them to take, the other person is easily confused about what you want and need. Rosenberg states, "Requests may sound like demands when unaccompanied by the speaker's feelings and needs" (2015, p. 73). Our goal is to communicate with clarity, compassion, and a desire for generative communication to occur.

Instead, choosing to pause before you speak gives you the opportunity to discover exactly what you want to ask for and why it's important to you. In this pause, you also can discover what might be important to the other person. Then together you can get creative regarding solutions without either of you abandoning self or hurting the other person in the process.

After someone expresses to you what they need, it's good practice to tell them what you are hearing. Now, what are they hearing you say? What are they thinking and feeling about what you said? Are they willing to move forward together honestly to find and implement a solution (Rosenberg, 2015, pp. 76-77)?

As you develop healthy communication patterns (habits) — connecting through the relational circuitry — you're able to listen for the feelings, needs, and values behind the other person's words and communicate your own clearly and kindly. You're widening and repaving the previously abandoned route through the thrive region, and eventually Route Thrive will be your default superhighway when you experience stress, or you will quickly be able to find the exit to this route.

There are myriad books on communication itself because of how vital it is in life. In this overview, I hope you have gained some awareness about the patterns of communication that are no longer serving you.

 **Withness Nugget:**

The best conversations happen when there is mutual intimacy; where all parties feel safe to share openly without fear of judgment or withdrawal of love. When we feel safe to be ourself with another person, we are operating from the relational circuitry of our brain. From this area of the brain, we connect with ourselves, others, and God in meaningful ways. How do I know if I've left the relational circuitry of my brain? Warner and Coursey tell us it's a piece of CAKE. It's an acronym they use to describe the characteristics of those operating in their relational circuitry. They describe the four identifiers as curiosity, appreciation, kindness, and eye contact.

Curiosity:

ON: I can feel curiosity about what people are thinking and feeling.
OFF: I do not feel curious about what others are thinking and feeling, nor do I want to or care.

Appreciation:

ON: I can feel appreciation in my thoughts and my body. I remember what I feel thankful for (gratitude), and I feel appreciation for the things, people, and moments I enjoy.
OFF: I feel resentment. I do not feel appreciation or gratitude, nor do I want to. I am focused on what bothers, annoys, hurts, tempts, or frustrates me.

Kindness:

ON: I can feel kind and tender toward others right now.
OFF: I would rather win and get what I want at this moment. I don't care how I come across to others. I have no desire to be kind.

Eye Contact:

ON: I look other people in the eyes.
OFF: I have no desire to look others in the eye. I avoid eye contact.

(Warner & Coursey, "The Four Habits of a Joy-Filled Marriage", noted in "The Joy Switch", Coursey, p. 52-53).

 **Mindful Moments:**

Practice sitting still with another human you are close to. Look at them intentionally in their eyes. Notice the color of their pupils. Notice their lashes. Now look deeply into their heart through their eyes. What comes up for you in your body when you have intimate eye contact? Is there discomfort? If so, where are you noticing this discomfort? Is there a feeling of connection? Does that feeling have a home? A temperature? A sensation?

How did this exercise impact your relationship?

**Journal Your Reflections:**

- Where do you find yourself on the journey to emotional liberation?

- What steps do you need to take to live 100% responsible to others and not for them?

- How can you communicate your needs, feelings, and desires so they will be heard and accepted?

- How can you stand boldly in the power of your voice?

# PRACTICAL APPLICATION

CHAPTER 17

# TRAUMA

---

"About 90% of the population has been exposed to a traumatic event, and 8-20% of those will develop post-traumatic stress disorder, or PTSD" (Treleaven, 2018, p. xvii). Individuals who have experienced trauma need to relearn how to find safety within their own bodies. Trauma survivors have trouble trusting their body's sensations and find that it provides them inconsistent and unreliable data. They often find themselves disconnected from their body from a sensory standpoint.

Let's dive into what is happening inside the body and mind of a trauma survivor.

Memory is recorded through two specific avenues: implicit memory and explicit memory. "Explicit memory has facts, concepts, and ideas attached to it, and this occurs when someone consciously thinks, either aloud or in one's head. Stories are housed in the explicit memory" (Rothschild, 2000, p. 29).

Implicit memory includes your subconscious — called "procedural memory" (Rothschild, 2000, p. 30) — think bike riding, teeth brushing, and driving. Implicit memory also includes stress hormones, emotions, disturbing body sensations, and behavioral impulses. These patterns can be activated subconsciously by a trigger. With repeated trauma, strategies for coping become habituated.

Episodic memory is an important part of the healing process. This type of memory is the bridge that connects implicit and explicit memories so that we can make sense of them and build coherent narratives. Healing happens when we build these bridges of meaning-making.

Within episodic memory, there are two subcategories. We know them as emotional memories and procedural memories. Our environment usually triggers emotional memories and manifests in physical sensations. Some of these physical sensations include chronic bracing, breath-holding, and tensing our muscles. These physical sensations need to be addressed when dealing with trauma. For example, if you suddenly feel rage or anger when you see someone walk into a room, it's likely your brain has made a connection in some way with a trauma you've experienced. These subconscious triggers can be activated by sensory stimuli (taste, smell, touch, sight, or sound) that the brain paired with the memories of traumatic events — this is called coupling.

Procedural memory is our how-to memories — think of the mechanics of driving a car. Within the procedural memory there are two responses: emergency responses (fixed action patterns such as fight, flight, and maintenance of territorial boundaries) and avoidance tendencies (Levine, 2015).

Why am I sharing this stuff? Because your body remembers. It absorbs the traumatic stuff and then activates certain patterns in your life. "Sensory inputs of traumatic events are encoded in your memory both explicitly and implicitly" (Rothschild, 2000, p. 44).

There are [a] few parts of the nervous system that are extremely relevant to those with trauma. These divisions are the sensory, autonomic, and somatic. The sensory is the root of our memory — everything begins with sensory input. This input comes from both external and internal sources and is transmitted to the brain for processing. "The two main sensory systems are the exteroceptive and interoceptive systems. The exteroceptive system receives input from outside the body by the eyes, ears, tongue, nose and skin. Interoceptors are the nerves that receive and transmit information from inside the body, from the viscera, muscles and connective tissue" (Rothschild, 2000, pp. 39-40). There are two major types of interoception: proprioception (kinesthetic sense of body part locations and states) and the vestibular sense (balance and posture in gravity)" (Rothschild, 2000, p.40). Your nervous system is regulated when you can toggle between these systems as a way of self-regulating and detangling some of these fused sensations.

Deep in the subconscious part of the brain, the neural circuitry determines if certain situations or people are dangerous or safe — this is called neuroception. In future encounters, your nervous system responds based on how you remember the situation or person, regardless of the accuracy of the memory. One might notice physiological shifts, such as feelings in the gut or heart, or an intuition that the context is dangerous. Neuroception also triggers physiological states that support trust, social engagement behaviors, and the building of strong relationships. "Faulty neuroception might detect risk when there is no risk or identify safety when there is risk" (Porges, 2017, p.20).

Back to my story in chapter 1. My neuroception evaluated the risk of the internal "heat" in the kitchen — my felt sense, intuition, and perception kicked in. Intuitively, it sent messages through my autonomic nervous system that signaled the need for my body and brain to jump into action. The reactions were automatic and subconscious; my body's reactions were physical signals that my brain needed to be on high alert and that I should mitigate the situation by eggshell walking (my learned stress pattern). This was my body and brain's response as I became emotionally dysregulated inside. I didn't know it, but retrospectively, dysregulation for me was showing up as stomach upset, heaviness in my chest area, and tightening of my jaw and neck muscles; I was physically bracing for the drama before I consciously knew there was a threat.

Trauma and PTSD manifest as a dysfunctional social engagement system in which a person's threshold for reacting — fight, flight, freeze/faint and fawn — via the sympathetic nervous system or dorsal vagal circuit is altered (Porges, 2017). "When we are in the window of tolerance, we [feel] safe and harmonious. Trauma survivors have a narrow window of tolerance, which can be expanded by expanding neural pathways" (p. 24).

Many of the neural connections developed in your youth have helped you survive your big-T or little-t traumas. Let me start by clarifying what trauma is. Trauma is often associated with those who have experienced war, combat, natural disasters, physical or sexual abuse, terrorism, catastrophic accidents, violence or life-threatening disease [—] usually something horrible that happens to us in a singular exposure. These are "big T" traumas. However, an accumulation of smaller or less-pronounced events can still disrupt emotional functioning and therefore be traumatic, but in "small t" form (Barbash, 2017; Rehman, n.d.). Trauma is when there has been "too much" "too soon" or "too fast" (Johnson, 2021, p. 36).

Little-t traumas are the more chronic or repetitive traumas, such as emotional abuse, bullying, harassment, divorce, ongoing financial concerns, non-life-threatening injuries, racism, or childhood attachment issues. Those who were raised in low-joy family systems may have developed some of the same techniques to safeguard themselves emotionally and/or physically as those who experienced little-t trauma.

What I want you to notice is that our learned reactions are how we met our needs in childhood. These reactions are how we protect ourselves in the face of trauma, difficulty, or distress. If your circumstances were extremely painful, you may have needed to shut down emotions in order to survive the painful stimuli. This is where our invisible influencers enter the scene. These are your characters that jump in from your episodic memory to save the day.

The good news is that your narrow window of tolerance can be widened with neuroplasticity and nervous system regulation.

This is where coaching fits into the trauma paradigm. Coaching is a process that helps a person move forward powerfully and intentionally in order to live the life he/she was created to live. And since most of the population has experienced trauma in some form, coaches must be trauma-informed so they don't further harm their clients.

Many coaching clients have already gone through extensive counseling and treatment for trauma, so this is not what we are referring to here. It has been proven that healing happens in a safe community. I use coaching groups to create a safe environment for growth. In this environment, I encourage my clients to show up with courage, engage, and shine the light of their brilliance and their imperfections, which can coexist. Only when we can authentically share and grow in a safe space will we know what it means to be known and loved for our authentic selves. In these groups, there is no fixing and no lecturing. We practice communicating with empathy, honesty, and vulnerability, and then we take what we learn into our real lives. By practicing vulnerability and safety, we learn to live in a place of unconditional love instead of fear. We develop tools to regulate ourselves and co-regulate with our peers. In this space, it is safe to be real and known.

Using concepts from somatic coaching and polyvagal theory, coaching can help clients feel "safe enough in their bodies to fall in love with life and take the risks of living" (Dana, 2021, p. 1). When we can learn to "befriend our nervous system" (Dana, 2021), we can really start living aware and conscious lives. Emotions are guideposts to our nervous system's state of being. The body's sensations that precede emotions and thoughts give us clues to the physiological responses — fight, flight, freeze/faint and fawn — when your nervous system is outside the window of tolerance. These physiological responses have a baseline of reactivity and response. For example, on the sympathetic track, you might have noticed that the fight response begins with irritation, moves to frustration, then to anger, and then to rage as the threat — or perceived threat — escalates, festers, or remains unaddressed. Why is this important? Because dysregulation can be activated in different degrees depending on the threat or interpretation of the perceived threat (Johnson, 2021, pp. 26-27). This is part of the polyvagal ladder or hierarchy– your nervous system goes up and down the ladder shifting through states in a predictable order.

One of my mentors, Amanda Blake, a master somatic leadership coach, states, "Embodied practice creates durable change, because it rewires your entire neuromuscular and creates new embodied patterns that affect your day-to-day actions. If you take the time to build muscle memory for key personal and interpersonal qualities, such as the ability to maintain composure, access compassion, resolve conflict, and act from care, those qualities become accessible to you for the rest of your life" (Blake, 2018, p. 248). Your trauma no longer needs to define you. You can rewire your patterns starting today.

According to polyvagal theory, the "autonomic hierarchy is the system built around three building blocks that work in a certain order and come with preset pathways" (Dana, 2021, p. 5). These building blocks are:

1. The ventral vagal system (aka the social engagement system), which helps us 1) meet the demands of the day, 2) connect and communicate, 3) go with the flow, and 4) engage in life. This building block aligns with the harmony section in the window of tolerance.

2. The sympathetic system is an anticipatory system. Energy fills the sympathetic system, keeping it on guard to mobilize for attack, escape, brace, and feel anxious or angry. It is the hyperarousal state of chaos in the window of tolerance model.
3. The dorsal vagal system is the shutdown system. When activated, we shut down emotionally/psychologically and just go through the motions. We have no energy, disconnect from others and life, lose hope, and give up. This is the hypoarousal state of rigidity in the window of tolerance model.

The aforementioned social engagement system includes the "ventral vagal pathway to the heart, joined with the nerves that control our eyes, ears, voice and the way we move our head. Our learned patterns influence this system in our nervous system, way back to our childhood days, based on the quality of connection, love and engagement" (Dana, 2021, p. 41) — think attachment theory. Through the social engagement system, "we listen for sounds of welcome, look for friendly faces, and turn and tilt our heads toward safety. Micro-moment to micro-moment, through our eyes, ears, voice, and head movements, our social engagement system broadcasts an invitation for connection with someone or sends them a warning to keep their distance" (Dana, 2021, p. 41). "When we are anchored in ventral safety and regulation, we are ready for connection. When we lose our anchor in the ventral vagal system, we also lose our capacity for connection" (Dana, 2021, p. 44). Our set point of this social engagement system is determined by our experiences. This social engagement system reads facial expressions and tone of voice based on our past and then determines if we should go toward or away from the person in question.

Daily we flow in and out of these states of being, depending on the sensory input from both internal and external means. As mentioned previously, the window of tolerance is narrow for those who have experienced trauma, which means they spend more time fluctuating in and out of harmony. Learning to befriend their bodies can expand the window of tolerance for those who have experienced trauma. We do this by noticing what is happening inside and outside our bodies and how our nervous system is communicating how it is receiving the input. By learning to work with and regulate your body's response to stimuli, you learn self-regulation. This is the most effective way to feel safe and secure within your body and your relationships, which builds resilience, or psychological flexibility.

Most trauma survivors live from a space of chronic dysregulated states, which feels normal to them. When there is peace and they stop operating on Route Survive, they may feel bored, easily irritated, or restless. If this applies to you, just know that this is a normal experience as you learn how to regulate your nervous system; it's a good sign that your body is rebalancing and traveling back to your parasympathetic state, where you can rest, digest, and build authentic relationships. These states can be fine tuned and expanded as we increase our vagal tone.

Let's touch on mindfulness and trauma. According to Treleaven (2018), trauma-informed mindfulness is imperative for clinicians who work with mindfulness-based solutions. Having the ability to notice when someone is out of his/her window of tolerance is mandatory for mindfulness professionals.

When we engage in embodied self-awareness exercises, there is a possibility of old trauma wounds being reopened. Blake reminds us that "meditation is widely regarded as beneficial, and it absolutely is. However, for trauma survivors, meditation can sometimes be contraindicated. In the quiet of focused attention, the body speaks more loudly, and sometimes intense, emotionally laden memories can surface" (Blake, 2018, p. 35).

The goal for the coach is always safety. We must connect to affect. Awareness that trauma and mindfulness can activate dysregulation is how clients make sense of what their body is doing. A trauma-informed coach takes note of these fluctuating states of being in their clients.

## GRIEF ABOUT YOUR TRAUMA

Grief is the act of honoring what is precious that has been lost. There is a sadness that we rarely allow ourselves to feel.

Brene Brown, in her work "The Gifts of Imperfection," states, "We cannot selectively numb emotions. When we numb the painful emotions, we also numb the positive emotions" (2010, p.70).

For some of us, there is grief over the things lost in childhood. The intimacy, love, support, innocence, and carefree childhood could be missing for you. If so, make space and grieve that loss with God—He longs to be with you through this healing journey. Grief does not look to assign blame or escape the pain but to truly feel the loss. God is faithful to take our ashes, our losses, and our pain and redeem them for something more beautiful than we can think or imagine. The journey is for us to feel certain things, acknowledge them, and put them in their rightful place. Focusing on what we lost and our ongoing pain figuratively puts them on a throne to be worshiped. We need to do the work to strip them of their power and transform them into an opportunity for beauty.

Now, some of you have experienced agony no child should ever experience. I get it. I did too. But when we haven't grieved the loss or processed our trauma, we remain a child with unmet needs. We remain a victim of our circumstances. Victims are never victors; life continues to be a long and hard experience. Victims create the same thing over and over because their brain always finds what it's looking for — in this case, the brain is looking for the familiar relational dynamics that wounded them. They attract other high-drama individuals into their lives — hurt people, hurt people. Like a moth to a flame, we draw this result toward us as the mysterious repetitive pattern unfolds.

This is our work: to become fully present to reality without being enslaved to our narrative. Realizing this was huge for me! It is a process that shifts how you live and how you think. I have not arrived, but I travel this journey with other women who know there is more to life than what they are experiencing. God is a God of abundance, and He has beautiful things in store for you when you open your eyes to new perspectives and possibilities.

For some, part of this process is forgiving others and yourself for things lost in your life. Forgiveness and grief are impactful in their own ways, but together they are a powerful and transformative experience. Forgive others for the harm caused or the care that was neglected. Forgive yourself for things you have not completed well or have left undone that have unintentionally harmed others. Forgive yourself for imperfections and acknowledge that there is only one perfect

One, and it is not you. Forgiveness happens when we allow ourselves to experience the full body emotions that may have been forbidden, and we arrive in the space where we are able to flip our beliefs about our reality and see that the opposite of our story of wounding can be equally true. This is a process of setting ourselves free from the shackles of our pain.

**Withness Nugget:**

As I began to write this section, I realized that your trauma may be fresh for you. You may not be ready to visit thoughts about God. Your thoughts about God might only be thoughts of anger. If this is you, please skip this section. I get it. As a multiple T-trauma survivor, I understand firsthand the journey of healing. It is personal and oftentimes slow going. The main point I would like you to consider during this time is that you are NOT YOUR TRAUMA; you ARE LOVED WITH AN EVERLASTING LOVE (Jeremiah 31:3) by the Creator of the world.

There are some core thought distortions about God and trauma that I'd like to address, but before I do, I'd like to remind you that God is for you, not against you (Romans 8:31). When God created humans in His image, He said that "it is very good" (Genesis 1:29-31). Humans were the crown of His creation. He loves you with an everlasting love and will never leave you or forsake you (Hebrews 13:5). These are biblical truths that do not change, even in the middle of trauma and heartache.

Many distortions of truth come into play when we combine faith and trauma. When your brain experiences trauma, it looks to make sense of it in some way. Some of the messages your mind might create to make sense of your trauma are "I'm not worthy," "I'm not loveable," "I'm not enough," and "I'm responsible for causing the trauma." These lies are stress patterns developed when being raised in an environment without secure attachment. Please see "The Power of Showing Up" on secure attachment (Siegel & Bryson, 2021). In order to survive, we try to make sense of dysfunctional situations, and this becomes the "truth" we live by. In reality, we're living by lies, such as "I am unworthy of love and protection from God" and "God is teaching me a lesson/punishing me/training me through this pain." These lies are thought distortions that do not serve you any longer. They were a means for you to survive a tragic circumstance, but they do not need to dominate your decision-making any longer.

These distortions of God's love and presence hold us back from truly connecting with Him, others, and ourselves in meaningful ways. The truth is that God gives man the power to decide good from evil (Deuteronomy 30:15-20; Romans 12:2). Humans often choose evil. Evil choices grieve God's heart (Psalm 78:40; Ephesians 4:30). The lies that we believe about God are our own distorted perceptions. God loves you greatly and will not violate your will to force you to love Him, nor will He violate evil choices by flawed humans. The story of Joseph, who endured abuse at the hands of evil men, is evidence of this. (Continued)

 **Withness Nugget:**

Continued...

But I am also reminded of how God redeemed these events. Genesis 50:20 reminds us, "You intended to harm me, but God intended it for good to accomplish what is now being done, the saving of many lives".

God will take all of the evil and all our circumstances and use them for good at some point in our lives. He does not celebrate evil or cause evil, and it breaks His heart. (Romans 8:18-39). We are not defined by our past experiences, and we get to renew our minds and transform our reactions to the internal and external stimuli an unfair life throws at us (Romans 12; Philippians 4). Every circumstance can be redeemed (Genesis 37-50; Lamentations 3:55-60; Psalm 107:2-3). Immanuel means God with us — He was with you then, is with you now, and will never leave you. We get to move toward integration and wholeness of mind, body, and spirit, taking fragmented pieces of ourselves toward wellness with God, self, and others. We get to experience and be with the parts of us that we have hidden or discarded as a survival tactic. We get to tap into the love portion of our brain and be with ALL parts of ourselves and God. This withness becomes a witness of His love and grace working in us and through us. From this place of withness, we get to walk in freedom, love, peace, and self-compassion.

### Mindful Moments:

Try these three exercises from Amanda Blake's book "Your Body Is Your Brain" to practice exteroception, interoception, and proprioception Please note: Proceed with these exercises only if it feels comfortable for you.

Exteroception practice: "Pause for a moment and notice what's in your direct line of sight right now. What's in your peripheral vision? Are there any smells in the air? Perhaps you didn't notice any a moment ago, but now that you stop to pay attention, you do. Are you surrounded by sound or by silence? Can you feel the texture of your clothes on your body? As I write this chapter (and many others in this book, truth be told), I'm enjoying the taste of chocolate. Perhaps you are enjoying something tasty too" (2018, p.45).

Interoception practice: "Get very quiet and still, and move your attention to the center of your chest. If you pay attention carefully, can you sense your heart beating? If you put your hand on your chest, does it become easier to feel? Perhaps you notice your lungs moving with each inhale and exhale. Is there warmth anywhere in your body, or coolness? Maybe you have a relaxed sense of spaciousness on the inside. Maybe there is tension" (2018, p.47).

Proprioception practice: "Get still for a moment. Without looking, do you know where your left hand is in relation to your left hip? Where your left foot is in relation to the floor? What direction is your head tilted?
As you are reading this, slump into your chair. Let your arms go slack. Let your chest collapse. Maybe drop your head a bit. Think of the last time you felt really down about something. Let that memory take hold for a moment.
Now say out loud, with as much enthusiasm as you can muster, 'I'm having a fantastic day!'

How was that? I'll bet your tone of voice is a dead giveaway about just exactly how 'fantastic' you do (or don't) feel. When I do this exercise in groups, people often burst out laughing at the obvious and ridiculous incongruence" (2021, p.53).

### Journaling Reflections:

- How have you tried to make sense of your trauma? Is that solution helping you or hurting you?
- What horrible circumstances have you experienced that were later redeemed?
- How can you learn to forgive yourself, others, and God for the trauma you have experienced?

### Nervous System Tracker

**Social Engagement System:**
What makes you feel connected?
What works to reconnect you with others?

**Sympathetic System:**
What makes you feel active?
What makes you feel chaotic?

**Parasympathetic System:**
When do you feel most calm?
What are your favorite go-to tools to calm your nervous system?

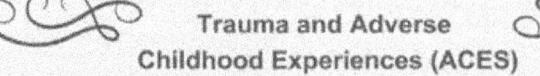

## Trauma and Adverse Childhood Experiences (ACES)

Trauma lives in your body — it affects your cells long-term — we can learn to rewire the patterns of reacting and choose more peaceful pathways as we seek to reset our nervous system.

"Childhood trauma increases the risk for seven out of ten of the leading causes of death in the United States. In high doses, it affects brain development, the immune system, hormonal systems, and even the way our DNA is read and transcribed. Folks who are exposed to very high doses have triple the lifetime risk of heart disease and lung cancer and a 20-year difference in life expectancy."

— Dr. Nadine Burke Harris, founder of the Center for Youth Wellness and current surgeon general of California

# Transform Your Brain

 **Sensory Grounding Using Touch**

Close your eyes if it feels comfortable to you. Begin with a few deep breaths through the nose. Breathe in on a count of 5, hold for a count of 5, and exhale for a count of 5.

Notice the rhythm of your breath.

Now gently rub two fingers together with such tension that you feel all the ridges on your fingers. Notice all the sensations you are experiencing. Your fingertips and hands have extra sensory cells that activate the thrive region of your brain.

Continue to breathe deeply and gently rub your hands together — noticing all of those sensations. Continue this exercise for one minute, focusing on the sensations.

What did you notice in your body, in your nervous system, and in your thoughts with this exercise?

CHAPTER 18

# QUIET QUITTING/ QUIET CRACKING

Harvard Business Review continues to talk about the quiet-quitting phenomenon. This is an extreme reaction to not feeling appreciated, acknowledged, or valued in your work, which leads to a low-joy environment and low job satisfaction.

The term "quiet quitting" was first coined by economist Mark Boldger in 2009. In the past, we may have said we are "checking out," "silent resignation," "living unconscious" This is where we settle for mediocrity. In this checked-out space, we are not present in our minds or in our work; we wear masks (figuratively) and show up to life with excuses, numbing all negative emotions. Quiet quitting is a form of resistance , where quiet cracking has to do with burnout. Gen Z feels most vulnerable to "quiet cracking." Quiet Cracking, unlike quiet quitting, is about survival." (Tim Elmore)

Quiet cracking is a silent deterioration of employee engagement and a surge of burnout –that eventually causes the worker to snap. This is a survival response.

To live with presence, you need to tap into the thrive region of your brain! Love, joy, peace, patience, kindness, goodness, faithfulness, gentleness, and self-control do not live in the survive region!

We experience the fruit of the Spirit in the thrive region, when we are connecting with the Vine; when we do so, we bear more fruit. In the thrive region, our thoughts become more like His thoughts.

The widespread cries of the phenomenon is indicative of the survive region of the brain being accessed by a majority of the population. I would like you to consider what it would look like if everyone addressed this quiet cracking by spending more time in the thrive region and learning to manage their nervous system.

If we stopped managing people from the nonrelational portion of our brain, the possibilities would be endless. If we approached how we lead from a relational perspective, we could all use our gifts and talents in the workforce and in the world.

Imagine the joy we would rediscover in our work and life.

Imagine the energy we would have left for the things that are most important to us if we weren't continually reacting out of the stress patterns that deplete our energy.

Imagine the possibilities for our world if we learned how to change our reactions into responses.

Life is a gift. Why would you want to live it unconscious and disconnected?

Why would you want to live your life without joy, without peace, and without the satisfaction and fulfillment of walking in your purpose as you engage in the world? Yet so many of us choose this daily.

When we live in the survive region, energy drains right out of us because of our fearful stress reactions.

We have no energy at the end of the day because we are living in the fear portion of our brain. Fear drains us dry, leaving us frustrated and focused on failure as our — by default — chosen lens of life.

When you live chronically depleted, it is evidence that you have not learned how to tap into your power!

You no longer need to live with chronic energy depletion. This is why I created the Micro-Shift Reset System® the experiential micro-learning system that uses gamification and brain based tools to build new neural pathways and habits. This system helps you gain awareness of your current state and shift out of survival mode without quitting your job or moving to a mountaintop. This Micro-Shift Reset System® empowers you to reset on-the-job, in real time, without disrupting your workflow. When combined with coaching, it's the secret sauce to reclaim control over your inner world.

 **Practicing Radical Self Acceptance**
adapted from
"The Stress Prescription" by Elissa Epel

For the tough things that you cannot change, consider this practice. Keep in mind, that whatever we resist, persists. Accept it completely, in your mind, your heart, and your body. Notice how you desire to resist accepting the thing you cannot change. Accepting it does not mean you approve of it. It is a choice to not expend your energy or lose your happiness because of it.
Imagine a situation that has already happened that bothers you deeply and cannot be changed — one that you find hard to accept.

Close your eyes and focus on your breathing for 2 minutes.
How might that situation be a blessing in disguise? What is the gift and opportunity that may come from that situation in the future? Are you willing to accept the situation for what it is and let go of the resistance to trusting that God has got your back? Acknowledge that there may be sadness or grief. Notice the sensation in your body. Put your hand on your chest, with kindness and warmth. Remind yourself that you can put down the weight you are carrying. It is no longer yours to carry. Consider your suffering as a human condition and have empathy and compassion for yourself. Consider the One who knows your pain and suffering — withness as a witness.

 **Emotional Processing**

Processing emotions takes less than two minutes and is good for your body and spirit. For the Bible scholars out there--this is not a New-Agey influence-- science backs this. There is a brain-body connection that must be addressed.

When I say processing emotions, I mean noticing the energy you are experiencing. Begin with some deep belly breaths, slow down your breathing, and pay attention to the energy. Bring your attention to where this energy begins in your body. What is the temperature of this energy? What is this energy trying to tell you? Is it alerting you to a threat? Is this threat real or imagined? Is the threat true, and can you really be certain that it is true? Who do you become when you respond to assumptions? Is there a boundary or value of yours that has been violated? Just get curious and don't judge yourself.

If you find yourself judging, implement a micro-shift reset and return to your thrive region of your brain where all good things happen. This is exploring your inner world and learning to challenge it. Often the Inner critic comes in to condemn you for feeling an emotion that you learned was off-limits. Remind yourself these are learned patterns and return your attention to the sensation. Notice when your inner critic shows up, acknowledge him/her, and tell him/her to step aside. Ask yourself questions and notice the gift and opportunity of experiencing this emotion fully. Give it a name. "Oh, this is just sadness. I recognize this emotion". You need to name your emotion for what it is in order to reframe it. Siegel says, "Name to tame it or reframe it" (2020b, p.) ( It's alerting you to the fact that something just occurred with another human being that has been painful.

Get curious. Why has this emotion triggered such pain? Where have you seen this emotion before? What stories are you telling yourself about this emotion? Are they true? Can you just be present with this emotion and ride the wave until completion? Can you just have compassion for yourself that you are human — and have just been triggered by a sad event? Soothe yourself like you would a toddler in distress. With a toddler, you would sit with them and just hold them for a minute until it passes. You would be present in their suffering. Sit with yourself and do not abandon yourself for expressing how you feel. Be present in the moment. You deserve the 60-second break it takes to feel the neurochemical release in your body as you soothe yourself.

Once soothed, the toddler gets up to run off to play. You are now ready to reenter with compassion for yourself and others. Notice that the others involved are just like toddlers with bottled-up, unprocessed emotions too. This is the human experience. Don't judge them, feel compassion for them. You can be this support for yourself and others. Just taking these holy noticing moments to mindfully connect to your inner world will change everything for you. It will conserve your energy and leave you refreshed.

CHAPTER 19

# MEDICAL PROFESSIONALS

I'd like to begin by saying thank you. Thank you for your dedication to serving humanity. Coming from a family with more than 12 family members in the medical field, I get what happens on the front lines. Most of us who enter medicine are compassionate and have high empathy; yet over time, we build internal walls to compartmentalize this part of ourselves. It is a survival technique, and it is not your fault. It is multifactorial, yet you already know this. Though glaring at us daily, the problems in medicine will not be the focus here. The focus for us will be on your internal landscape and managing these challenges with a new lease on life.

For starters, survival mode leaves us cynical and judgmental. This is the role of the survive region. It judges people, places, things, and circumstances. It is infused with negative emotions and filled with shame, blame, guilt, and anxiety. In this region, you will find your saboteurs ruling your thoughts, feelings, actions, and behaviors. There is good news. You can shift to a more productive area of your brain, which will help you return to joy.

During medical training, we work and study long hours to be at the top of our game. It has programmed us to put aside our own needs and emotions. We forego food, water, and bathroom breaks and wear it as a badge of honor. Meeting everyone else's needs is top priority, and busyness often equals success in our minds. Many medical professionals have an eerie discomfort with sitting still because it is foreign territory. No wonder we are running on empty and totally exhausted!

Add the global pandemic to the mix and we are ripe for stress patterns to reign. Before we jump into these stress patterns, I'd like to address the elephant in the room. The elephant's name is "unprocessed emotions." We've got doctorates in stuffing our emotions! We've neatly learned to put our emotions in internal boxes, quickly shutting the lid, and hoping they stay put — but they don't! Emotions don't follow our dictates. Unprocessed emotions are like stubborn toddlers digging their heels in and expecting to be paid attention to. Emotions will go to great lengths to be seen and heard. They will even lodge themselves in specific body parts until you pay attention. They cause diseases and symptoms you are already familiar with because you're treating them in your patients and recognize them in yourself. Your invisible influencers like to distract you into blaming other things for your physical pain; however, it is often these stubborn toddlers throwing their tantrum in your body.

Emotions beg you to pause and interpret the data they are providing. You've convinced yourself that you don't have time to process emotions, or that this is too touchy-feely and "I'm logical and scientific." Keep in mind, your opinions are just sentences your brain tells you. The truth of the matter is these sentences keep you stuck in dependence on your saboteurs and your stress patterns. Emotions scream for your attention and will not stop until you acknowledge them. Like toddlers sprawled on the floor, your emotions beg to be noticed.

Your busyness is a neat distraction from processing emotions, but it is the very thing that will drive you toward burnout and away from wholeness. This busyness keeps you from showing up as your best self for your family, patients, and colleagues. It keeps you distracted and double-minded. Emotions are like waves — they have a peak and then they fizzle out! When they are peaking is when we immediately want to push them away. Resist the urge to do this. Learn to stay with the wave. You cannot surf it if you do not stay with it. Dr. Jill Bolte Taylor, a Harvard brain scientist, states that "[w]hen a person has a reaction to something in their environment, there's a 90-second chemical process that happens in the body; after that, any remaining emotional response is just the person choosing to stay in that emotional loop. According to Taylor (TED, 2008):

"Something happens in the external world, and chemicals are flushed through your body, which puts it on full alert. For those chemicals to totally flush out of the body, it takes less than 90 seconds. This means that for 90 seconds you can watch the process happening, you can feel it happening, and then you can watch it go away.

After that, if you continue to feel fear, anger, and so on, you need to look at the thoughts that you're thinking that are restimulating the circuitry that is resulting in you having this physiological reaction, over and over again. And we can all choose whether or not to stay in that thought loop."

Take the 90 seconds necessary to process your emotions! Your nervous system will thank you.

In medicine, life is one big emergency. Everyone has needs, and adrenaline pulsates through our veins as we address these emergencies. We've all experienced a coding patient who required our all, only for our efforts to not succeed in saving them. We immediately move to the next patient, especially in our emergency departments. This is a mistake. We must make space to process what just happened. We lost a human life — someone's mother, brother, child, or friend who was loved. There is now a void in the world because of this loss. Take a moment to honor that life and honor the work you and the team did to try and save that life. Acknowledge that you are not God and do not hold life in your hands. Acknowledge that you did your very best to save this person, and take a moment to let that emotion run its course. Silently thank God that He knows best and that He remains on the throne, even when you feel you failed. Note: This feeling of failure comes from your invisible influencers and the inner critic. Quickly bring yourself back to the thrive region of your brain, maybe choose a micro-shift from the micro-shift reset system.®

Sit silently for 90 seconds to two minutes and acknowledge these truths in full emotion. Thank Him for the role you were privileged to play in the patient's life. Thank Him for the bond you have shared with your team, where all differences were put aside to work together toward saving a life. You harmoniously produced a piece of music as a team that has ended like an operatic tragedy. Remember your position — you are not God, but you get to be used by God. Be present in this sacred moment and honor the life, death, and unity before you, in the witness that will be a witness to those around you. This is presence. This will feel different and satisfying when you finish your day, because you did not trap it in your body and lug it home with you. It's a burden to carry unprocessed emotions. Emotional weight piles up and becomes too much to bear. Instead, you are taking two minutes to be present. Once the wave has passed, you may move on to the next crisis, fully present to the next patient and the team.

When you quiet your mind, expand your heart, and remain present in your body, you are functioning as a complete person who is interconnected with those around you.

If you want this and don't know how to do this in real life, I found an app (The Pause app, by Roundglass, at https://appadvice.com/app/the-pause-app/1482649724) that was created by an emergency room nurse who saw the need and stepped into the gap to fill it. It provides a quick process that you can invite your team to step into with you. It's 15-30 seconds of silence in which you honor life and the team and show gratitude and appreciation for all who did their best.

In your work, you face hardship daily. Thank you for stepping into the pain of real life. Our country got a taste of the effect of real-life tragedy during a frightful medical emergency with Damar Hamlin, live, on a televised NFL football game. The emotion experienced by our country was palpable. People dropped to their knees and Facebook blew up with pleas for prayer — I posted a plea too.

As we watched the emergency unfold, I thought of you and the weight you carry daily. It is tempting to block out the heaviness of your work, but then I am reminded of Brene Brown's words again: "We cannot selectively numb emotions; when we numb the painful emotions, we also numb the positive emotions" (2010, p. 70). If we want to live fully present, we cannot choose to numb or stuff the painful emotions. We must learn to process them fully and allow ourselves to feel. Emotions are a human experience. We are humans before we are medical professionals, moms, friends, sisters, or brothers. Allow yourself the space to be human.

Your work is a beautiful privilege with holy-noticing moments everywhere. We need to operate on Route Thrive rather than Route Survive. You can experience joy in your work and life, even when painful moments are a regular occurrence.

Right now I hear you saying, "Emotions are taboo in the workplace." I call nonsense! Those are just sentences we have told ourselves on repeat that trap us in our little boxes of perceived safety. Sentences like this are causing physical and emotional pain — they must be disrupted! We must put new sentences in their place. This is the work that needs to happen to live a full and anchored life. When you step into this inner work, you will experience life fully and have a peaceful presence, even in high-stress situations.

Pretending that the emotion doesn't exist just fuels its existence. The internal pressure continually increases until it explodes. The explosion is the problem, not the emotion. That pressure will remain contained without effect (or, at least, we think there's no effect) for only so long. It must be examined either now or later.

When I say "process your emotion," it doesn't even need to be out loud to start. You can just create a moment to feel the emotion through the whole wave. Eventually, find a trusted friend to do this work with you. Learning new ways of processing and experiencing your emotions will help you return to joy quickly and expand your window of tolerance. It all begins by noticing, pausing, and breathing. When we approach these emotions with curiosity instead of judgment, they don't feel as threatening. We get to explore what is behind the big emotional charge for us. There is always something driving the emotion. Many times it's an old pattern that is no longer serving us. This is our growth moment — when we get to choose the exit ramp to a new highway.

**Thought Monitoring to Shift Your Suffering**
**Adapted from Byron Katie's *The Work***

Is it true?

Can you absolutely know it's true?

How do you react internally and externally when you believe that thought?

Who would you be without the thought?

Turn the thought around: (what truth can you put in its place)?

Examine your thoughts: Think about the things listed in Philippians 4:8-9. What other Biblical Truth can you reflect on?

 **Withness Nugget:**

You were called for a unique purpose to support others in medicine. Who you are and what you do matters! It's actually ingrained in your soul and part of your being. Self-regulation mastery is the most effective way to reclaim joy, peace, and purpose in your work. When we can connect with ourselves we can affect others through the power of Christ in us (the hope of glory, Colossians 1:27). You are not alone in your work; He is with you in your high-stress environment. He desires for you to turn to Him. He created your nervous system, and He can help you regulate it. "The Lord Your God is in your midst, a mighty one who will save; he will rejoice over you with gladness; he will quiet you by his love; he will exult over you with loud singing" (Zephaniah 3:17, ESV).

He sings over you, He rejoices over you, and He will quiet you by His love. Experience His love and reconnect to Him from the thrive region of your brain.

The legacy that you leave is your choice. You can continue to walk in your divine purpose in medicine and receive His quiet presence. You can also quiet yourself when you begin to feel dysregulated. "I do not occupy myself with things too great and too marvelous for me. But I have calmed and quieted my soul, like a weaned child with its mother; like a weaned child is my soul within me" (Psalm 131: 2, ESV).

You can love your career again when you connect with God, others, yourself, and your purpose. The stress of the career may not change, but God has the ability to change you from the inside out. He actually delights in this work. You can be strong AND in need of God. You can be brilliant AND imperfect at the same time. His love can overflow in and through you as you practice the work you love. You can recover from the symptoms of burnout and fatigue. You are strong and capable, and you can learn to self-regulate and turn to the One who knows. "Trust in the Lord with all your heart and do not lean on your own understanding; in all ways acknowledge Him, and He will make your paths straight" (Proverbs 3:5-6).

 **Mindful Moments:**

There are so many moments in medicine to savor; these are the moments you live for, and these are the moments that make a difference in the world. You have the unique blessing of being with others on some of the worst days of their lives. They are in a crisis situation, and you are the expert in the crisis. Being the expert does not make you exempt from self-care and self-regulation. When the pressure begins to build, what tools can you choose to ground yourself and be present in the moment?

How can you shift out of the future and into the present moment? What can you appreciate in this moment? Who can you connect with in this moment? Look into the eyes of your patient. What do you see?

**Journaling Reflections:**

- What area of your life needs to be shut off so you can recalibrate your nervous system (i.e., Your phone, home access to the EPIC system)?

- Where do you gain refreshment and rejuvenation? How can you build more of this into your schedule?

- What triggers at work activate your survival reaction? What steps can you put in place to shift from Route Survive to Route Thrive?

- How can you step into your leadership at work and create a state of co-regulation with your co-workers? How can you lead from a regulated nervous system?

## CHAPTER 20

# ON BURNOUT

---

There is a movement happening in our midst — a movement toward the wellness of medical professionals worldwide. I've interviewed over 60 experts and thought leaders in the stress management, and organization psychology world to bring you current practices and trends in healthcare.

Coming from a family of medical professionals, I am passionate about providing options for these professionals to love their work and lives again. It's time to rise above the stress patterns and reclaim your life, energy, and joy. You can find information about my work with healthcare professionals on my website. https://www.doreensteenland.com.

These speakers have been nothing short of inspirational providing their best tips for success. One visual stood out to me that I'd love to share with you.

Many of us are running on empty, and we think this is normal. We use the phrase "this is a marathon, not a sprint" to remind ourselves that we are in this race for the long haul. This phrase reminds us to slow down, but it does not include stopping. Dr. Rola Hallam brilliantly pointed out the flaw with this thinking (2023). When thinking about a marathon, you run without stopping for long periods of time and often face exhaustion. This is not how we want to live our lives. She points out that we want to live our lives like a relay race. In a relay race, we run hard for our portion, then pass off the baton to the next runner so we can rest.

She pointed out another flaw with the marathon analogy: You are going it alone. But in a relay, you have a team. You were not created to go it alone. Brilliant! I never saw the flaw with the marathon analogy until this interview, and now I have a new mindset on the race that we are called to run together. This is the power of conversing with other like-minded people on the same journey. Learning from others shows why group coaching programs are so transformational. We learn best from the stories of others because they help our brain make new connections among our neural pathways. This one is a beautiful visual I will carry with me on my journey.

## YOUR BRAIN: THE CONNECTION MACHINE

Remember, your brain is a connection machine, and these connections are on- and offramps in your brain's neural pathways. The more connections you can make to a new truth, the more ramps you are creating. Your brain automatically chooses pathways at high speed. When you are trying to create new habits (take different pathways), it's imperative to create as many ramps as possible. These become high-speed ramps between pathways. These ramps combine old memories, sensory stimuli, times, places, people, emotions, and events. When we link familiar stimuli with the new pattern, it creates more-appealing (or less-appealing) routes for future travel.

James Clear, author of "Atomic Habits" (2018), talks of a habit loop in the brain. The brain's habit loops are in response to getting a reward (on-ramps) or avoiding pain (offramps). Your brain decides what is good or bad depending on past rewards or punishments. It catalogs the rewards as good and wants to repeat them. The problem begins when your brain puts a situation in the wrong category. This happens all the time because your brain doesn't know better. This loop gets cued by stimuli, which leads to craving the reward, which kicks off the release of chemicals into the bloodstream. Once the trigger cues your brain, you experience a craving (usually emotional energy), which leads to a reaction or a response. If the reaction or response is what the brain decides is good — BAM! — you've gotten a reward.

Let's play this out in an example. You get off work at 5 p.m. after a stressful day (umm, most days in medicine, right?). Your brain has determined that to relieve your stress, you need a drink of alcohol. You have a drink, and it relaxes you. Your brain now links alcohol as a solution to stress. Please note that your brain doesn't discern if this is a suitable solution; it just recognizes you wanted to relieve your stress and the alcohol relaxed you. Because of this momentary stress relief, your brain puts alcohol in the "good" category. Pay attention to what you allow your brain to tell you about your solutions.

So the next day at 5 p.m., your brain sends a message: "Hey, you have stress, and it's 5 p.m. Have a drink and relieve this stress." The cue is the stress and the time! Your brain made a connection — left a mile marker — associated with 5 p.m. Clear teaches that the cue or trigger can be the time, a location, a person, an emotional state, or a preceding (or succeeding) event (2018). You experienced stress, you had a drink, and the resulting stress relief rewarded your brain with a dopamine hit. What you may not know is that alcohol does not cause relaxation — you just think it does because it slows down brain functioning. It actually causes the exact opposite because of how it affects dopamine levels. Without getting technical, alcohol increases anxiety and the craving for more alcohol. What a horrible habit loop to get caught in!

Next time you reach for a drink to relax, notice that you will start feeling relaxed as soon as you pour the drink — even before taking your first sip! Your brain reports to the chemical centers, "The loop is complete; release the reward!"

When you listen to your brain like this, you may end up drinking too much, gaining weight, and being dissatisfied with your decisions. This creates a self-sabotaging cycle because your actions and plans do not match. Cue the Judge, who steps in to manage this situation with shame, guilt, condemnation, or anxiety. The Judge thinks it's motivating you to do better, but it's really not your friend. The Judge is a poser!

You can disrupt habit loops like this by inserting new mile markers along the way. The markers are really just triggers that throw you on a pathway automatically. This is helpful if it's a ramp to pathways that serve your needs and values; if it's not, you've got to create new, better mile markers.

(An offramp is created the same way. Let's say after you have that first drink that first day, you lose your balance, fall, and hit your head hard enough you need stitches. You just dropped a mile marker that alcohol makes you wobbly and you may fall, and that's definitely not fun. You now have an offramp when your brain suggests alcohol as a solution to your stress!)

Your brain wants to link memories, smells, sights, situations, and conversations to your habits. These mile markers are ramps to/from pathways. Be intentional with them. Coaching speeds up your growth by helping you link new connections and thoughts to old memories and thoughts.

This sounds hard, but it's really not. It is about learning to be intentional. It is about being present in the moment. This is not la la land ideology but neuroscience at work. fMRI studies show us exactly what happens in our brains and how we build new neural pathways.

As medical professionals, we wear a badge of honor as helpers and healers. This badge does not exempt us from caring for ourselves, and it should not send us into hiding. We are leaders, and leaders take action. Leaders proactively solve problems; they don't wait for the ship to sink. If you feel like your boat has a leak, it's time to step up and lead yourself. It's time to be proactive and get help from a coach, counselor, or colleague. There is no shame in needing someone else to illuminate your blind spots. Your brain runs in patterns and biases, just like everyone else's. These are best seen by nonjudgmental outside observers. Let the eyes of someone impartial help you bring your life to the next level. This is what leaders do. Leadership, as defined by Amanda Blake, is someone who "cares deeply, [focuses] on creating a new future, and [has] skills to collaborate well with others" (2018, p. 103). You are a leader, and leaders commit to discovering their blind spots so they can lead well.

You have created a legacy of healing, hard work, and dedication. How would it feel to add deep, meaningful relationships to that legacy? What would it feel like to be fully present with your family? How would it feel to know others and be known by them? You can learn how to be brave and vulnerable. With some practice, you will notice a renewed energy and joy when you get real and begin self-leadership. You can learn to move these changes from head knowledge to your heart quickly with experiential, transformational coaching — I would love to assist you!

## BURNOUT AND THE SYSTEM

Just a few clarifying words here. There is often shame associated with experiencing the symptoms of burnout. It is not your fault as a practitioner. It is not a weakness in your character. This is a reaction to a system that is malfunctioning. It is a reaction to repeated, unprocessed trauma. Throughout this book you have received tools to manage your inner landscape. These tools are important for your well-being as they empower you to become a catalyst of change in your environment. You are leaders in your profession, and leaders inspire change. These tools are to equip your internal landscape for the leadership you will need to demonstrate to right this sinking ship.

Let's start by defining some symptoms of burnout. Those who experience burnout syndrome have a crushing level of exhaustion. This is not the normal exhaustion that we all have from time to time when we have had a full and straining day. This is crushing, inescapable, and chronic. It comes with cynicism and apathy toward your patients and/or colleagues. It is a feeling that you are ineffective and not making a difference in the world any longer, so you withdraw mentally from your work and your passion. There is a depletion of joy as you operate from the survive region of your brain. Joy cannot exist here. The chronic high-stress environment drains your energy and drive.

It's important you know that you are not the problem. The system is the problem. Dr. Christina Maslach, University of California, Berkley and creator of the MBI (Maslach Burnout Inventory), and Michael Leiter, an organizational psychologist, have identified six forms of organizational mismatch in their book "The Burnout Challenge" (2022). Lacking alignment in any of the following indicators increases your risk of burnout syndrome.

These indicators are "work overload, lack of control, insufficient rewards, breakdown of community, absence of fairness, and value conflicts" (Maslach & Leiter, 2022, pp. 6-7). These are the areas on which you should focus as you endeavor to lead change in your environment. Notice today how these areas are showing up in your work environment.

The system of personal development I use as a coach helps you strengthen your own sphere of control and connect with others, self, and God more deeply. As humans, we give away too much power to things outside our control. Coaching can help you live in alignment with your values and clean up the lens of your perceptions. Personal development helps you conquer the stress patterns that keep you stuck in the same old reactions. When you make these changes, you will have new tools to call on in your most challenging moments. The internal changes will affect your influence in your external environment. If we desire a seat at the problem-solving table, we need to put our oxygen mask on first.

This chapter's focus is you. Not because of weakness, brokenness, or a need to be fixed, but because your stress patterns have you playing small.

There are plenty of great works on organizational leadership and restructuring, but this is not one of them. My current favorite is Brene Brown's Strong Ground, if you haven't read it, get it immediately. This book is for you and your personal development. Consider it personal CME credits accrued by stepping into your power.

All change starts with awareness and must be from the inside out. It is time to heal ourselves so we can continue our important roles of healing others.

I hear your objections from my kitchen table — "I don't have time." Physical, emotional, and spiritual illness do not wait for you to have time. You will either take time now to heal, or your body and/or mind will break down and force you to take time later.

Stress patterns and trauma are weighing you down. It's time to care for yourself. It's not selfish, it's mandatory. Without caring for yourself, the accumulation of stress will rob you of joy and leave you with regret. When you rewire cruise-control reactions that keep you in survival mode, you will recover the joy you once experienced in your career. All it takes is a first step — you are worth it.

What is the legacy you desire to leave for your family and your coworkers?

 **Withness Nugget:**

You were called to this profession as a healer. Your calling is irrevocable.

When you get discouraged and fatigued, remember your calling. Remember the values that drew you to medicine. Remember that you, your team, and your patients share a common humanity with the Creator of the world. The work that we do in medicine is a privilege that allows us to be with others in some of the most tragic times of their lives. We get to be the light and love of Christ that they need in their moment of distress. Yet as healers, we cannot pour from an empty cup. He has come to give everyone abundant life. When we remain anchored to the source of our strength, we can heal compassionately from a place of overflow, not scarcity. We heal others and ourselves best from a place of wholeness and integration.

**Mindful Moments:**

5,4,3,2,1 — Exercise to Regroup Yourself Anywhere: When you begin to feel yourself leaving the window of tolerance and need to regroup, practice this exercise.

Begin with a few deep calming breaths, if this feels good to you to activate your vagus nerve. This tells your body it's time to rest and digest. Now, when you are feeling more calm, list five things you can currently hear. Notice four things you can see, and really notice the intricate detail of those things. Now bring your attention to three things you can touch. It might be a different texture or temperature, or it could be your fingertips rubbing together. It might be washing your hands and feeling the warmth of the soap and water. Notice the sensations. Bring your attention here. Now list two things you can currently smell and one thing you can taste.

Notice what you discover with this exercise and journal it.

 **Journaling Reflections:**

- What are your current stress cycles that interfere with your work-life satisfaction?

- What lies have you been believing about medicine that might need to shift?

- What patterns are you noticing? Reflect on your body and record any new sensations you notice, putting descriptive words on paper. Where in your body do you notice this sensation? Is there tension or weightlessness? Temperature changes? Is there a feeling or numbness? Notice your patterns from a place of curiosity, no judgment is allowed.

- What are the current tools that you use to navigate stress and beat exhaustion? Are they still serving you, or do they need to be updated?

### Heart Coherence Breathing: Heartmath Institute

What is heart coherence breathing? It is breathing that calms the nervous system and brings one into harmonious order, stability, and connectedness, where we function as our best selves and have the ability to use energy efficiently. It occurs when our body's systems, breathing, heart rhythms, brain rhythms, and hormonal responses are in sync with each other.

### Exercise

Take a moment and focus on your breathing. As you breathe, notice if you are breathing from your nostrils or your mouth. If you notice, mouth breathing, please switch to nostril breathing to activate all the extra benefits of this exercise.

As you inhale through your nose, focus on your heart area in the center of your chest. I'd like you to breathe a little slower and deeper than usual. If you'd like, you can put your hand over your heart to help keep your focus there.

Imagine your breath is flowing in and out of your heart or chest area. Imagine the oxygen flowing out into your heart and out through your body. Just breathe slowly and gently in through your heart and out through your heart area. Do this until your breathing feels smooth and balanced — not forced. Continue to breathe with ease until you find a natural rhythm that feels good to you.

As you focus on your heart-centered breathing, make an attempt to experience a regenerative feeling, such as appreciation, gratitude, or love for someone or something you care about deeply. This could be a feeling of appreciation or care for a special person or a pet. Or try to focus on a place you enjoy or an activity that is fun. Our goal is to re-experience that feeling. Allow yourself to feel it as you focus on your breathing and the positive regenerative experience.

Just hold the intention of appreciation or care. Imagine with each breath the experience of adding energy reserves to your energy bank. After you've activated a positive feeling or attitude, you can anchor it in as you continue your heart-focused breathing.

## Glimmers

As humans, we have a built-in negativity bias as a survival response, and negative experiences carry more influence in the brain than positive ones. We get to actively be looking for the positive experiences in our lives because the brain will always find what it's looking for. What are the micro moments that make you feel good? It could be a sunrise, the stars or moon in the sky, a bird, the smell of fresh flowers, the touch of a soft blanket. A glimmer could be anything that shifts you to a space of calm, balance, and joy. They can be predictable or unexpected moments during your day. Stop, notice, and take them in. Fully experience them.

What glimmers can you notice today? Ponder them; experience the sense of safety and calm that comes with them: and actively choose to look for them. When you see your glimmer, practice gratitude and thanksgiving.

 **Can I Drop the Rope?**

"When I catch myself trying to change something that's not in my control, I take a moment and visualize it as though I'm pulling a rope that's tied to something immovable, like an enormous boulder. I'm using up all my energy trying to solve something that cannot be solved. That rock will never budge. I gently ask myself:

**Can I just drop the rope and let it be?"**

("The Stress Prescription", Elisa Epel, p.47)

 **Naming Your Present-Moment Experiences**

At this moment I am feeling (emotion), and I am sensing in my body (list three body sensations). What does this situation remind you of (do not revisit all the details, just acknowledge the connection and shift back to the present)?

At this moment I am noticing my breathing is (be descriptive about your breathing pattern — such as chaotic, smooth and regular, deep and slow, fast and shallow).

Which tool might you choose to regulate any sensations, emotions, or patterns that are not serving you?

CHAPTER 21

# THE POWER OF PRESENCE:
## LEADING FROM A PLACE OF AUTHENTICITY

---

## THE SECRET BEHIND EXECUTIVE PRESENCE

Most people think executive presence is about how you look or how well you can fake confidence. But it's deeper than that. It's about how you *show up*—your authenticity, your energy, your calm—in every moment, especially when the pressure's on. True presence starts in your nervous system. When you can regulate your internal world, you lead with clarity and composure, no matter what's happening around you.

Executive presence is often treated like a mysterious quality—something leaders are told they *should* have but rarely taught *how* to build. It becomes a vague reason for a missed promotion or a piece of feedback that feels impossible to define.

Here's what I believe: **executive presence is nervous-system-friendly leadership.**

You've probably heard the advice to *fake it till you make it*. The problem is, faking it creates internal conflict. It suggests presence is something you *put on*, like a costume. But real executive presence comes from the inside out—it's *embodied confidence*. It's not about performance; it's about presence. When you lead from authenticity, people *feel* it. They can sense when your nervous system is grounded, and they can also sense when it's not.

That calm, clear steadiness? That's your superpower.

## THE ANATOMY OF PRESENCE

Executive presence is made up of several connected qualities that build authentic leadership from the inside out. At its core is **authenticity**—being true to who you are. Your team, colleagues, and even your family can spot pretense instantly. Real leaders lead from their strengths and stay comfortable in their own skin. Authenticity builds trust and gives you confidence to navigate hard moments without losing yourself.

Closely tied to authenticity is **self-regulation**, a key aspect of emotional intelligence (EQ). It's your ability to stay calm, centered, and effective under pressure—especially in fast-paced environments like healthcare. When your nervous system stays balanced, you think clearly and express emotions appropriately. Lose that balance, and your leadership influence slips.

Then comes **self-awareness**, the ability to notice your emotions and understand how they impact your actions, mood, and team. Emotionally aware leaders recognize when they're tense, triggered, or distracted—and make micro-adjustments before those emotions spill over. They see their strengths and limits clearly and keep a growth mindset, learning instead of reacting. They lead with confidence but don't take themselves too seriously.

Emotional intelligence also shows up in how you work with people. I like to call this a **coach approach to leadership**—skills like active listening, asking powerful questions, reading verbal and nonverbal cues, and influencing through empathy.

**Empathy** is the superpower that will never be outsourced to artificial intelligence. It lets you see from another's point of view, balance perspectives, and keep the bigger picture in mind. It's how leaders create trust, inclusion, and connection across differences.

Leadership isn't just about strategy or results—it's about *people*. When you can read a room, understand what others need, and connect on a human level, you build loyalty and safety. This is where empathy becomes part of the culture. People perform better when they feel seen, heard, and understood.

Adaptability ties it all together. A leader with executive presence can pivot when things change without losing focus. They stay attuned to their environment and people, moving with the room instead of against it. This kind of **psychological flexibility** allows you to recover quickly from setbacks and adjust strategies when needed. Calm, resilient leaders naturally inspire confidence.

Another vital piece is **clarity and focus**. Great leaders cut through the noise, tame their inner critic, and communicate with precision. They recognize patterns, connect the dots, and bring order to chaos. When you're clear, your team becomes clear.

Leaders who operate within their "window of tolerance" can manage strong emotions and stay composed under stress. This stability sharpens their decision-making and communication. It also helps them navigate conflict with steadiness instead of defensiveness. Simply put, clarity creates calm.

And finally, **value-driven behavior** is the glue that holds it all together. Integrity, fairness, and candor are non-negotiable. People trust leaders whose actions match their words. When they don't, confidence breaks down. Authentic confidence happens when your *insides* and *outsides* match. If they don't, it creates cognitive dissonance—a tug-of-war inside that everyone around you can feel.

## WHY IT MATTERS

In healthcare and high-stress workplaces, burnout is at an all-time high. Leaders with strong executive presence set the tone for how their teams handle pressure. When you lead from presence—calm, grounded, emotionally intelligent—you create a nervous-system-friendly environment where people feel safe to perform, even on their hardest days. Your regulation becomes their regulation. You model composure, and that steadiness ripples through your team, your patients, and your organization.

## BUILDING PRESENCE WITH THE MICRO-SHIFT RESET SYSTEM®

The key to developing executive presence isn't about becoming someone new—it's about using tools that help you be your best self *on demand*.

That's where the **Micro-Shift Reset System®** comes in. Think of it as your real-time toolbox for rewiring your brain and regulating your nervous system. Each micro-shift helps you return to calm, clarity, and connection when the pressure hits.

A quick breathing reset between patient rounds.

A pause before delivering feedback.

A one-minute grounding exercise before walking into a tense meeting.

These small, deliberate shifts interrupt old patterns of stress and replace them with new, sustainable patterns of presence. Over time, they don't just change how you lead—they change who you *are* as a leader.

The Micro-Shift Reset System®, combined with coaching and practice, helps you move from reactive to responsive, from hurried to intentional, from tense to composed. You begin to lead with your full self engaged—body, mind, and spirit aligned.

## WHERE TRUE LEADERSHIP BEGINS

When you master the art of executive presence, you unlock a form of leadership that's not just effective—it's transformative. You stop leading from survival mode and start leading from stability. You exchange hustle for presence, control for clarity, and performance for authenticity.

And that, my friends, is where true leadership begins.

# CHAPTER 22
# PARENTS OF TEENAGERS

◆

### COLLECTING TREASURES AT THE SHORE!

Living on the east coast of the United States affords me daily glimpses of the power of the Atlantic Ocean. As the tide ebbs and flows, it often leaves things behind on the shore. The objects come in all shapes and sizes, each one unique in its own right. For instance, look at the shells on the sand — some are perfect, some are shiny, some have an intricate design, some are smooth, some are rough, some are colorful, some are dull, and some are cracked. Each shell is beautiful and unique, with its own story of origin.

Some objects will remain on the shore, where someone can collect the treasure. Other objects are swallowed up and whisked away by the raging waters before anyone can catch them.

These treasures are our teenagers — the future of our society. We need to collect the treasures on the shoreline before the raging waters wash them away. Make no mistake, the waters are raging, and they will not stop raging. The stakes are high.

These treasures fueled the passion for writing this section of the book. Our teens are experiencing pain right now, and it's a pain that goes unnoticed because we are busy keeping up with the frantic pace of the world. Our teens do not have the tools necessary to tackle the demands on their hearts and minds without discipleship, mentorship, and empowerment, and too few people invest in the next generation regarding the matters of greatest importance.

There is a collective heartache experienced as a society when we write off an entire generation within our culture. The treasures are screaming to be unleashed on an unexpecting world. Our young adults are full of untapped creativity. Their minds are full of ideas, dreams, solutions, and innovations that are caught in the raging waters. Our teens need help to get to shore. "The purposes of a person's heart are deep waters, but one who has insight draws them out" (Proverbs 20:5).

I write this from a place of love, redemption, and gratitude toward God for His work in and through me, as I was one of these teens, and now my kids have stepped into the world of "real jobs." Our teens need people of wisdom to listen to their genuine struggles and concerns so that the tides don't whisk them away. Will you be one of those people for the next generation?

How do we collect the treasures before the raging waters consume them?

To identify a solution to a problem, we must first understand the problem. As with most problems, it isn't pretty. Please hang with me through this hard part so that we can get to the good part and the hope it can bring.

As I watch the rise in teen suicide, self-injury, addiction, and mental illness, my heart breaks for these kids. We have somehow failed to see them, failed to hear them, and failed to understand them, and it grieves my heart.

Our society has fallen into traps of consumerism and striving. They are lies that we have been ingesting ourselves and feeding our kids. We teach our kids that if they work their fingers to the bones in grammar school, high school, and college that they will have a high-paying job upon graduation, when in reality many graduates are jobless and full of debt, anxiety, and hopelessness. We have pushed the thought that if they have the perfect college resume they will get into the perfect school and then they will land the perfect job, only for them to graduate unemployed. Worse yet, many find themselves tens of thousands of dollars in debt and they still have not found their passion.

Cultivate your treasure!

In pushing them to have the perfect college resume, we have neglected to discover their passions and unique purpose. The minute we discover a sport that they have fun playing, we immediately turn it into a full-time job so that they can pursue a scholarship in the sport. The result is our kids do not enjoy their sports. What should have been fun, exercise, and joy in the process has turned into work and identity.

Cultivate your treasure!

What's the problem with hard work and dedication to a sport? By placing such great importance on these things, they become the teen's identity. Any parent whose child has been on injured reserve during his/her senior year of high school understands what I'm saying. One injury, one global pandemic, one bad coach, one missed cut – you get the idea. Building their self-worth and identity in this way fosters a victim mentality when their identity is ripped away. With the recent global pandemic, as all the activities came to a standstill, the rates of suicide, anxiety, and depression among teens skyrocketed.

We need to rethink the messages we are sending to our young adults.

Cultivate your treasure!

The next contributing factor to the increased incidence of stress-related symptoms is the constant stimuli of technology. There is no white space in their minds or calendars to learn how to think about their thinking, to dream big dreams, to discover their creativity. If they have ideas, they lack the fortitude and time to carry them to fruition. Our kids do not know how to be still and know that He is God or sit at His feet to hear His marching orders.

Cultivate your treasure!

We have not trained our young adults to deal with uncomfortable thoughts and emotions. Placing them in bubbles, we have protected them from any discomfort. We fight their battles for them as if they were incapable of standing up for themselves. It is time to shift our thinking.

Cultivate your treasure!

These well-intentioned maneuvers to help our kids be the best and do their best and to keep up with the Joneses are not only exhausting for us and them, they have robbed our kids of any joy in life and created a perfect storm of mental illness that is already abounding.

Cultivate your treasure!

We have replaced the importance of church with all the things we think our young adults need to compete successfully in this competitive world.

Our churches have even shifted. Our churches were once places of grace and acceptance — hospitals for the hurting — but that's no longer the case.

When interviewing young adults for this book, it was fascinating to hear how they see our churches. Remember, these are general impressions of how young adults see church — this isn't a reflection of all churches, and your opinion may differ.

Here's my summary of what they said:

- Church is a place where they should be seen, not heard, and they should be submissive right away!
- Church is a place where adults place more of an importance on rules over relationships, programs over people, and perfection over process.
- Church is a place where as soon as they connect with a youth leader, the leader moves on, so they resist connecting.
- Church is a place where they are not free to challenge adults'/the church's thinking.
- Church is a place that does not address the cultural challenges without the adults in charge feeling threatened (it's not a safe place to become critical thinkers).

- Church is a place where they do not have choices or room to breathe.
- Church is not helping them make hard decisions for real life.
- Church makes them feel like they don't belong when they have doubts about things.
- When they walk into church, they feel like they're being judged or that they're damaged.
- Church leaders have higher standards for them than they are currently living in their own lives (hypocrisy).

And it's not just our churches that exasperate our teens. Our political leaders resort to name-calling, shaming, and blaming, dividing us instead of unifying us. Elected officials vote their party lines, without regard for what is actually best for their constituents. Selfish motivations and hidden agendas drive their policies. They cannot engage in healthy communication, resolve conflicts, or collaborate to find the best solution for the most people. They will plow over anyone and anything that gets in their way. These "leaders" care more about their stock portfolios than equality for all men and women. They lack moral conviction because they do not know the Truth. They've exchanged the Truth of God for lies. Slander, gossip, dishonesty, discord, selfish ambition, and vain conceit abound. Thanks be to God that where sin abounds, grace abounds all the more (Romans 5:20). We know this to be true, but it sure doesn't seem that way when we look at society.

In the absence of humility and repentance, we get more broken promises, more identity confusion, more isolation, and more hopelessness.

Technology – biased news – more lies – more cynicism. There's fear that if one speaks the truth, someone will cancel them. Censored speech. Hatred of Christians. Racial injustice and oppression.

All of these equal a mass exodus of youth fleeing the church that has left them with no answers to their hard questions; the future of our society is fleeing God because He is being inaccurately represented by His people.

So many of them are asking: "What is the Truth?" "Has it all been a lie?" "Who can I trust?" "The adults in my life have misled me. Where can I turn?"

Google and AI would love to answer your teen's questions. Why? Not because they care for your teen, but because they care for their agenda. We can do better.

My concern is that the problems seem so big to us that it is easier to numb ourselves with scrolling, shopping, eating, and drinking. As adult influencers, we're handing our influence over to the raging waters — social media, the internet, their peers, etc. The growing legalization of marijuana across the country certainly shouldn't be a surprise. The "adults" seem perfectly content to pass our responsibility for raising our children to anything and anyone. We make excuses by saying we're too busy or by staying distracted to ease our own discomfort and hope that our teens will turn out alright. This also shouldn't be a surprise: it's not very likely they will. And the reality is Satan is the only one who benefits here.

No one has more influence than parents, and you don't want your influence to be neglect, unrealistic expectations, shame, or any other relational dysfunction that pushes your teen into the raging waters. As parents, we must boldly and fearfully step into our teens' lives. Of course, not all parents will step up, so other adult influencers must. We have been called for such a time as this. We have been called to step out by faith, even when those steps are scary.

But we're stuck in our own stress patterns, so when it comes to engaging with our children, we do one of two things: We either search for an excuse to avoid any discomfort, or we become pseudo dictators within our homes. Both result from our stress patterns, and the long-term effect is that we perpetuate the cycle — our children are developing their own fear-based stress patterns because we can't deal with our own fears.

We need to look at the saints who have gone before us. Their faith was not based on comfort. Their faith was not based on a certain outcome or even on having all the facts. They took action based on their faith in the One who holds the stars in the skies. It took courage to act when it was scary. And frankly, if there is no fear, it would not require faith.

We want our kids to be well-adjusted Christ followers who are authentic and who live as lights in the world although the struggles are real.

We want them to be Christ followers who have the hard conversations that need to happen and who aren't afraid to take their light out of the bushel. People who show up with love and kindness and admit that they don't have all the answers but they know the One who does. People who are comfortable being uncomfortable. Christians who choose not to use the Bible as a defense mechanism but as something that helps them offer genuine support and presence. Christ followers who listen and ask curious questions as they seek to use their God-given creativity to solve problems. Christ followers who are comfortable meeting people where they are at, instead of regulating thought and choice.

But we can't expect our teens to be this type of Christ follower if we aren't setting the example.

What if we showed up in love and kindness as Christ modeled it for us? What if love and kindness were the very things that lead our teens to repentance (Romans 2:4) and the thrive region in their brains?

Remember, this verse follows the verses with all the bad stuff we do as members of fallen humanity, such as exchanging the truth of God for a lie and worshiping and serving created things instead of the Creator (Romans 1). We see it throughout the world and rail against it, yet we are blind to the ways we are prisoners to it because of our stress patterns. We often stick our heads in the sand or demand blind obedience because we are afraid of relationship and vulnerability — our thrive pathways laying unused and in desperate need of maintenance.

We need to say with Paul that "[we are] not ashamed of the gospel, because it is the power of God that brings salvation to everyone who believes" (Romans 1:16). Paul reminds us he is "obligated to both Greeks and non-Greeks, both wise and foolish" (Romans 1:14). Later on in the book, he tells us they cannot believe if they do not hear (Romans 10:14-15). Are we not at least obligated to our own children?

So if we are obligated and responsible to our children, let me ask you a question: Are you ever willing to listen to someone who ignores you or someone who wags their finger in your face and tells you what you must do? Not likely.

We expect them to just get it because we do and we go to church or we "share" the gospel with our teens in a combative and authoritative way. Imagine if we engaged in rational discourse with them, devoid of shaming, blaming, and name-calling, right where they are. What if we were mindful, truly listening to them so that we would know where to meet them? What if we were curious instead of judgmental? "But God showed His own love for us in this: While we were still sinners, Christ died for us" (Romans 5:8). He died for them too, just like He did for you and me.

If we believe it is God's transformative power and His "kindness that leads one to repentance" (Romans 2:4), then why do we abdicate our responsibility or step into God's role as judge and jury of the heart?

I remember as I first entered the church as a young 20-something. I had lived a lifetime of stuff before my arrival into Christ's family, and with that stuff came a lot of rough edges. Many of those rough edges were apparent by the way I dressed, in the way I spoke, and in the way I interacted with others. I'm thankful for the grace I received, because I could not have endured seeing all my stuff at once. You can't either, and neither can your teens!

God acts in integrity with His character — He is love (1 John 4:7-21). In the New Testament that love is called *agape* love, and in the Old Testament it's called *hesed* love. "*Hesed* runs deeper than social expectations, responsibilities, fluctuating emotions, or what the recipient deserves. The message of the gospel —

God's act of forgiveness and salvation in Jesus — is rooted in *hesed*. *Hesed* describes the disposition of God's heart not only toward His people but to[ward] all humanity. The love of God extends far beyond duty or expectation" (Vine, 1996) (italics added).

To help adult influencers approach the next generation as gentle guides who are committed, fearless, authentic, and loyally and patiently loving — like Jesus — who invite rather than push, control, and mandate change, we need to view it through the lens of a biblical worldview, adopt a coach approach, and seek help from neuroscience that is supported by Scripture.

This segment is about exploring deep connections with others, self, and God and using this relational connection to change our world for Christ. We will look at a holistic approach to parenting as we tackle the body, mind, and strength aspects of parenting with our entire self.

Get on your life preserver, because we are about to enter the raging waters with our teens!

## SWIM SCHOOL WITH THE MASTER INSTRUCTOR!

Have you ever experienced a relationship with someone where you felt fully known, fully heard, fully accepted, and loved unconditionally? It's a rare thing, so when you discover it, you don't want to leave it or lose it.

God is relational. We are made in His image. Jesus came to reestablish that relationship with us both here and in heaven. Throughout these chapters, we have discussed the concept of withness. This concept is what the gospel is all about. I referred to John 15:11 as we discussed withness: "I have told you this so that my joy may be in you and that your joy may be complete."

For the past 20 years, neuroscientists have been expanding their knowledge of the brain. They have discovered how the brain and body work together holistically. The discoveries have been mind-blowing because of the recent advances of fMRI studies and advanced scientific research.

Relationships, parenting, and marriage are the schoolhouse where we get to implement these tools. God gave us the ideal place to practice responding to emotional triggers — it's called the family. You know, the dirty dishes left in the sink, the snarky attitude from your teen, the kids who do not listen to you when you speak, the rule follower who wags his finger at you, you fill in the blank … you know, all the triggers. All the choices and all the opportunities God handpicked for you for your sanctification! God picked your kids for you too, and He knows you are the perfect parent for them!

It's in the holy-noticing moment that we get to choose sanctification or sin.

This is the moment we get to choose between survival brain and thrive brain, between disconnect or presence.

When triggered, we get to choose our response. We get to choose to respond with God or react without Him. When we choose the latter, the part of our brain that runs on cruise control takes over and we react in many habitual ways: yelling, withdrawing, fighting, fear, anxiety, eye rolls, or door slamming. These reactions hinder our relationships and our connection with those we love.

When the part of our brain that empowers us to connect with others is activated, we can respond to the triggers WITH GOD AND WITH OTHERS, thus deepening connection and decreasing division in our homes. This secret area of the brain has been asleep for many of us, but we can activate it. When activated, we can recover quicker from triggers, we can stay connected with others during stressful times instead of pulling away or numbing our emotions, and we can call on and actually feel God in the middle of the mess.

"The thief comes to steal, kill, and destroy. I have come that they may have life and have it to the full" (John 10:10). In my business, I help people find this fullness with God, others, and themself. Again and again my clients tell me how they desire peace and joy in their homes, how they feel their teens pulling away, and how the disconnect is painful. One of the developmental milestones for adolescents is to spend less time with parents and more time with friends. This is a completely normal part of them learning to live in the world without us. However, this distance often triggers parents negatively, which just increases the tug of war between frustration and control. We can learn how to BE PRESENT WITH GOD AND WITH OTHERS in the middle of this tug of war by tapping into the joy Jesus has always desired for us to have.

When we choose to react, we shut down and then they shut down, and our relationships, peace, and joy suffer. When we choose to respond from our relational circuitry, we get to have a mutual mind moment — that special awareness of us, the other, God, and the energy we are all producing. Through coaching, you could explore how to apply this to your daily life and empower the next generation to leave its footprint of emotional and spiritual wholeness in society.

Parenting teens is messy and hard, but we can meet our kids where they are so that they can experience the messy grace of the WITHNESS AS A WITNESS TO THE GOSPEL OF JESUS CHRIST.

## DON'T SWIM ALONE!

Imagine for a moment it's early in the morning and you're alone in a body of water. No one knows where you are. It's quiet and beautiful. The silence is deafening, but the tranquility of the morning is a great time to think. In this unrushed and undisturbed place, I went windsurfing. Yes, me! Mind you, it was a younger me, but it was me!

I was new to this activity and my skills were very basic, so I wanted to learn and practice in a relaxed and private way. I had worked the night shift as a nurse and was supposed to be home sleeping, but I wasn't tired, so I hopped on my board and headed into the water.

It was majestic, and things were going well — until the wind shifted. As a beginner, I didn't plan for this, so I was struggling to get myself headed back to shore. My anxiety increased as my attempts to turn myself around were only bringing me further out to sea. Nothing I was doing was working!

Then it happened — I got caught in the tidal current, and panic struck me in a big way. Now I was being pulled out even further and quicker! Alarmed, I remembered I was alone and had not told anyone where I was going. I was alone on the sea and had no control. It would be 12 hours before anyone would even think to look for me, and I had no way to send an SOS. I was so afraid of drowning!

BUT GOD came to my rescue again! It was not the first time He had saved me from calamity, but this time He made Himself *known* to me.

God sent a boat out of nowhere! The boat was far off, but somehow it saw me and noticed that I was being pulled out to sea. This kind man came to my rescue. He towed me back to the safety of the shore, where I could put my feet on solid ground. Boy, was I thankful! As I thought about it, I remembered His faithful hand throughout my whole life, and this sparked my personal love story with God. Our relationship did not begin there, but I would come to remember His faithful provision during that crisis. Now, looking back, He had been wooing me to Himself for years, but that had gone unnoticed.

As parents of teens, we've all experienced the tidal current of emotion pulling us out to sea. The winds are gusting and the waves are crashing. What used to work for us as parents is no longer working. Just like I felt the sense of alarm as the current uncontrollably pulled me out to sea, parents experience these emotions when they sense an ever-widening chasm between them and their teens. We once had control, and we were windsurfing in the gentle breeze of parenting. But then the wind shifted, and the current overwhelmed our abilities to navigate the rough waters ahead.

How many of us try to figure things out on our own when it comes to parenting, just like I tried to figure out windsurfing on my own? "Unrushed," "undisturbed," "relaxed," and "private" —

sure, this environment is a great place to learn, but environments like this are normally this way because they're controlled. What in the world makes us think anything about parenting in this fallen world will be controlled? Why in the world don't we reach out for help when the winds shift in our relationship with our teens? Cue the Schoolhouse of God for moms and dads!

God loves us abundantly, and our growth and development is front of mind for Him. This is our opportunity to grow, to learn, to develop new skills, and to learn to lead from a place of courage instead of fear. He doesn't ask us to go into the waters alone — that would be as silly as my adventure. But He has given us our unique child to grow us in the specific ways He has deemed necessary, and for us to grow them. It is here that we get to choose withness or to go it alone and continue the way we have always done it.

As we explore new possibilities, I'm asking you to approach our conversation from the perspective of a beginner. I fully understand that many of you are seasoned parents. No doubt you desire excellence for your kids, like all good parents. But I'm asking you to come with a curious heart and mind, as if you've never done this before in your life.

Don't let your brain get defensive right now. Put the brain drama aside and let's get curious together. Learning new things usually feels very uncomfortable at first. Lean into the discomfort. Learn WITH God and lean into Him. He is our ultimate teacher and desires that we openly listen for His still small voice. God prompted me to write this message when I had no desire to write a book, so I know it's important. We will leave the application of the message up to each individual family because God is not about cookie-cutter parenting. Lean back on Jesus' chest, like the disciple Jesus loved (John 13:1), and listen for his heartbeat. Listen closely to His voice whispering the truth to your heart.

 **Withness Nugget:**

As we parent our young adults with God, I'd like for you to consider how God approaches you. Let's think about it: Jesus — Immanuel, God With Us — came "while we were still sinners" (Romans 5:8, NIV), not to condemn the world (John 3:17, NIV) but to save us from ourselves. He parented us with love, full of grace and truth (John 1:14), and did not offer that love based on our behavior--the Pharisees were living proof of this.

Yet, as parents, we often get wrapped up in the externals. We find ourselves drifting with the world's ways of parenting instead of meeting our young adults where they are at. Jesus connected with those He affected, and we must do the same. Often, our own insecurities and baggage from childhood come with us to our parenting, driving our anxious comparisons. It is as though we are protecting our own reputation and identity above training our young adults to manage their internal turmoil.

God is with you. God is with your young adult. Your young adult has questions. They have big emotions that they are having trouble regulating. In order for them to co-regulate, they must feel safe with you, and you must feel safe with them — this is a prerequisite. As I think of this withness principle and Jesus, I believe no one questioned His love for them when He was in their presence. He gave His full attention to whomever He was with. They experienced His love deeply, and it moved them to follow hard after Him. He was totally present in all of His interactions. Jesus used a coach approach with His parenting of us. He knew that change from the inside out required buy-in from the person needing change. He was present — God with us — He asked curious questions and then gave the recipient space to breathe and the support to work through the questions with Him.

**Mindful Moments**

Dana states, "Connection brings a sense of relationship. The experience of connection encompasses four domains: connection to self, connection to other people (and pets), connection to nature and the world around us, and connection to spirit. When there is a rupture in our sense of connection (losing our sense of self, experiencing a mishap in a relationship, being cut off from nature, or becoming distanced from our experience of spirit), our ability to anchor in safety and regulation is challenged, and we turn to communication and social engagement to try to find our way back into connection" (Dana, 2021, p.12). Being present and connecting with your young adult is how they begin to mature and learn to regulate and be present for others.

Visualize a time when you felt connected, safe, and regulated in your relationship with another. Sit with this internal picture for a while. What does it feel like? Where do you feel this in your body? Is there a temperature that accompanies this feeling? What needs to happen within you to achieve this state with your young adult?

 **Journaling Reflections:**

- What internal motivation keeps you from showing up empathetically for your young adult? Is it fear? Is it your reputation? What is it for you?

- What truths from the Bible have we possibly misrepresented or misinterpreted when we consider parenting?

- What steps would you like to take to self-regulate and be present for your young adult?

CHAPTER 23

# WAVE WATCHERS: LISTENING AND OBSERVING THE WAVES

―――――◆―――――

"The first act of love is the giving of attention."
**― Dallas Willard**

My town is on the Atlantic Ocean. Beautiful old homes with large front porches (the favorite part of my home) and perfectly manicured yards sit on tree-lined streets. From the center of town a train line runs north to New York City, and the train's horn blows regularly as it crosses the intersections. The seashore is lined with a two-mile boardwalk that we get to walk daily for exercise, and there are two peaceful lakes and a pond.

We have town parades, tree-lighting ceremonies, festivals in the town center, and a small theater. It's a walking town! Daily you see people walking their dogs, walking the boardwalk, and walking through town. This was the draw for me as I was considering where I would raise my family.

Did I say how blessed I am?

There are sounds in this environment that others might notice that I no longer hear. For example, that train. It blows its horn throughout the day and night; it has become such a familiar sound that I only hear it when I'm trying to notice it. Even the crashing waves can go unnoticed unless their rhythm changes.

Another sound is the alarm that sounds to notify our volunteer first responders to man their vehicles and get to the station quickly. The number of blows of the horn gives them the information they need about the situation before they arrive. This is another one of those sounds that most of us are able to tune out, but that's not the case for everyone. The volunteer workers are always listening for that alarm. They are intentionally alert so that they can jump into action when they hear it.

Our homes can become like these familiar sounds. Our home and the people in our home are familiar, and sometimes we tune them out. It happens when we let everyday distractions drown out the sounds of those we love the most.

What if we chose to be like the volunteer workers, tuning our ears to the voices of those in our homes? Being intentional about our interactions is required. It takes observation skills. It takes courage to turn off cruise control and learn to be present for others and to discover withness.

As we approach learning how to ride the waves of parenting teens, we need to hone our observation skills. So for one moment, come with me to the ocean. See the sparkling water reflecting the sun's rays, notice the seagulls diving for fish, and feel the sand between your toes. Now, tune your ears to the sounds of the waves. What do you notice? What sounds are you noticing in your mind's eye? Now notice your home environment. What are the waves in your home like right now? Are they huge and crashing? Smooth and tiny? Are they chaotic and without rhythm?

There is a rhythm in your home. Fine tune your observation skills and notice it. Think deeply about this rhythm. Does this rhythm sound peaceful? Is it a rhythm of grace? Or is your home filled with tension? Some families describe the rhythm of their home as heavy metal rock 'n' roll with a band screaming loudly in the background. Others use jazz — filled with complex harmonies and lots of improvisation and irregularity — to describe their home. This is just an observation period. Just observe, without judgment, the rhythm of your home.

Next, let's observe the current: What is the current in your household right now? This is often much more difficult to detect. The waves are what we see on the surface; the current is all the stuff happening underneath it. It's the motion of water within the ocean. Deep-water currents are like underwater conveyor belts and are hidden to the naked eye. Temperature, wind, and salt content affect the current.

How is the wind affecting your current? Is it a soft and refreshing gentle breeze or hurricane-force winds?

What is the saltiness of your home? When I think of salty, I'm thinking of Christ followers being the salt of the earth (preserving, enhancing flavor). However, society is now using salty in a different connotation. Our teens are using the word salty almost interchangeably with being irritated, angry, or annoyed. So what is the salt level in your home, and which description would you use — the Christian description or your teen's?

How deep is the water in your home? Are you struggling to keep your head above water? Or is it so shallow that there is no room to wipe out safely?

You are probably saying to yourself, "What's the big deal?" I'd like to remind you we are learning to surf, and all these things contribute to successful surfing. As parents of teens, we often focus on the surface level — the outward attitudes and behaviors. What we don't seek to know or understand is what is really going on under the surface. We will go into this more in depth later, but for now we are noticing. We are becoming wave watchers!

As wave watchers, we are collecting data. We cannot change our home without having the correct data, so this is where we are at right now. We are observing patterns in the waves, current, and tides. What are you noticing?

You are here right now because you have poured your life into your family, and you love them. They are disconnecting and pulling away from you, and it's scary. It makes you want to cling tighter … I get it. But that only increases the resistance we experience. What we are talking about doing here is learning how to reconnect to our growing kids without turning into helicopter parents, and step one is noticing!

As we become expert wave watchers, I'd like you to consider how you are listening. Really pay attention, because this is the number one complaint of teenagers: "You don't listen to me!"

There are many levels of listening, and how we listen affects our relationships on many levels.

Let's explore some of the listening styles. Before we begin, I want you to know that we are all guilty of drifting in and out of all three types. Just like we are becoming wave watchers and learning to observe the waves and the current, we are going to learn to observe our listening. Listening is one of the major keys to a) learning how to ride the waves of parenting teens, b) having great relationships, and c) affecting others at work and at home. As we notice how we listen, we will deepen our connection and presence with those we love and everyone we interact with. Remember, our withness is our witness. The more we can be "with" people, the more we can impact them positively.

## DISTRACTED-MAMA LISTENING

Listening only halfway defines this level of listening. You know what I'm talking about. This is the listening we do when we are listening for facts and information while we are on the computer, cooking dinner, or scrolling on social media. When we use distracted-mama listening, we are filtering out all the fluff and listening only for what we need to know or only what pertains to us. We may or may not be engaging with our eyes, and our body language is screaming, "Leave me alone!"

Sadly, this is the level of listening so many of us live with. Your focus (and that of others in your house) is on self and your inner dialogue. The result leaves us and our loved one's feeling lonely and unseen. Notifications and a million things that surround us distract us. We've trained ourselves to work in a state of multitasking, and we've told ourselves that it's good. I'm here to tell you what you're doing is not multitasking, and it's not good.

What is multitasking? Multitasking is when we are doing many tasks at the same time with a single focus. Let's use driving a car as an example. When we drive a car, we are checking the rearview and side mirrors. We're using our blinkers and looking at the road ahead of us as we follow the directions to our destination. This is multitasking, and it all has the same focus — driving. When we multitask like this, it is not harmful. It is our brain's way of doing things on cruise control. Your brain is conserving energy and working efficiently. You don't even need to think about these things to do them.

Multitasking is helpful when used in scenarios similar to the above. However, with handheld computers, we have become master switch-taskers. Switch-tasking is what we do when someone is talking to us while we jump to social media, then we jump to email, and then we jump back to the conversation. Not only does it have devastating effects on our relationships, it overloads our brains and leaves us feeling confused! Every time we switch tasks, our brain leaves behind an attention residue, which is like a foggy cloud. "This attention residue decreases our productivity by up to 40% and leaves us functioning as if we are stoned" (Oberbrunner, 2021).

If we are honest, this is the type of listening we do most as busy parents, and it's the type of listening our teens are doing regularly. This type of listening will never produce connection and depth in our relationships; this is NOT WITHNESS LISTENING. It's passive listening — not listening with intentionality. The telltale sign that this type of listening is active in your home is the blank look on their face. It's almost as if they are staring out into space, and it's the foggy residue that results from switching our attention back and forth to unrelated things.

It may show up for you if you have to ask about details repeatedly that your teens have already disclosed to you (guilty as charged!). You may hear from them, "Mom, I already told you I will not be here for dinner." Oops ... this is your clue that you were using distracted-mama listening — someone was talking and not being heard.

This type of listening can show up in another way as well. It shows up when we hear one word and cling to that word and jump into fix-it mode! When we are in fix-it mode, all we see is the problem at hand; we neglect to see the person on the other side of the problem. We resort to telling and/or yelling, then jumping into action without having all the details. Have you ever been there? I know I have! This is a fear-based move by our brain from Route Survive. We hear a word and it triggers some kind of automatic response.

Hey, this is the stuff I work with my clients on ALL THE TIME, so you are not alone. This is when our brain fills in all the gaps with our own data from the memory center in our brains. Truth be told, most times this data is inaccurate to the situation at hand and gives us more problems than solutions. The cool thing about our brain is that God made it so that we can train it and rewire it to cooperate with us in the listening process. I love helping my clients work through this concept.

Parents, these statements aren't here to induce guilt but to bring awareness to some of our patterns of interacting with our families. We cannot change until we know that there is a problem.

Our world has changed drastically, and we have been adopting its changes into our relationships. Sadly, the effects are being felt by all. We are exhausted and overstimulated by things that are leaving us feeling empty inside. We are running races God never intended for us to run. Living in chronic distraction overstimulates our brains and exhausts us, leaving us feeling empty inside and resulting in relationships without depth. If we want to leave a legacy and impact our young adults, this will be ground zero for us to rebuild a healthy foundation for withness as a witness.

## WAVE-WATCHER LISTENING

The second type of listening is an active listening style. It focuses on the other person and understanding. This is the type of listening that people walk away from transformed. They know that they have been heard and understood. Their circumstance may not be different, but their relationship with the circumstance certainly is, because now they know they are not alone. This type of listening focuses on the person speaking, not the listener! This is a monumental shift, because we are often thinking about what we will say next, and this is an obstacle for being a master wave-watcher listener!

When we employ this type of listening, we are giving others the space to hear themselves think. As parents, we often forget how the brain works to solve problems and move toward change. When we are listening with wave-watcher listening, we are "observing the non-verbal cues, the tone of the voice, the pacing of the sentences, the pauses in between, the hand gestures and the eye movements" (Williams & Menendez, 2015, p.5). This type of listening requires concentration and focus. Your phone is down, your eyes are up, and you are not in problem-solving mode. Sometimes we forget the people in front of us and look only at the problems. During this type of listening, it's okay to make "brief comments or ask clarifying questions" (e.g., "Wow, that sounds like it was a big deal" or "And what else"?), but opinions and demands are off-limits. Here's a simple example.

Repeat a phrase your teen says.

Teen: "I'm angry at my teacher."

Mom: "You're angry." (Then be silent and wait.)

This type of listening doesn't jump in to solve the problem; it creates a space for your teen to process the problem and to think and create new possibilities. You create a nonjudgmental, safe place for them to process, and then allow them to think it through.

A conversation is like a tennis match. Your teen says something to you (they serve). You return the serve with a brief, nonjudgmental statement or a clarifying question, then you wait for them to return the ball to your side of the court (volley). As parents, we are often like ball machines set at high speed! We hurl about 20 balls in rapid succession at our teens! Our brains cannot process so much information at once, let alone think. It's no wonder they get frustrated with us and lament, "Mom, you're not listening to me." Our brain can only handle about four things on center court (center court = prefrontal cortex — the problem-solving part of the brain) at one time (Rock, 2020)! What we need to remember is that they are already coming to the conversation with things on their court, so our job is to keep our sentences and comments short so they have the space to process and problem-solve effectively. These facts are true for all brains; however, you need to give even more grace to your teen's brain because it's still under construction!

## WAVE-RIDER LISTENING

This listening type is the withness listening type. It's not listening *for* information or listening *to* our teens. We are listening *with* our teens and listening *with* the Holy Spirit. Your entire focus is on energy, using your senses, and listening for God's voice. As your teen is speaking, you are attentive and engaged. You are praying and asking God to be a part of the conversation. You are seeking God's wisdom and prompts.

You are listening for the attitudes, emotions, beliefs, and mindsets behind the words — the undercurrents — that may not be serving your teen, as well as for any disconnects (to explore, not to fix). You are listening for hopes, dreams, frustrations, and energy, and you're watching for nonverbal cues. This is deep listening, and with this type of listening comes deep connection. This type of listening takes intentional presence.

You are able to access that intentional presence through holy noticing. What is holy noticing? Holy noticing, according to Stone, is "noticing with a holy purpose God and His handiwork, our relationships, and the inner world of thoughts and feelings. It is a way to bring intentional awareness in the present moment to what and who is around us and what we're doing, thinking, and feeling — all from God's perspective. – It is noticing the space between the stimulus and our response[,] which helps us have the space to think and feel differently so that we have the freedom to choose the best way to solve problems" (pp. 32-22; 16-17). It is in withness that we connect with God and others and choose our thoughts, feelings, and responses that will please and glorify God.

With wave-rider listening, we are partnering with God, so we HEAR what our teens are saying. According to Gary Collins (2009, p. 103), we are listening for:

H – hopes and dreams about how things can be better.

E – energies and passions that appear to inspire the person, but also the energy drainers that pull the person down.

A – attitudes and abilities that impact how one sees potential for the future, but that might be squelched or frustrated in the present.

R – routines, habits, and ways of doing things that may need to be changed.

It's at this point I think we need to take the time to discuss what wave-rider listening means and what it does not mean.

Wave-rider listening is listening with your teen to understand the Holy Spirit and your teen, calling on the wisdom from above. This type of listening helps bring awareness to discrepancies, mismatched values, and the things that don't align with your teen's goals and dreams. It's listening to help your teen gather more information and perspective than he/she had before they spoke with you. It's listening without judgment, without fixing, without telling, without lecturing, and without attachment to the immediate outcome, because you are trusting in a BIG God who changes hearts!

Wave-rider listening helps your teen feel seen, heard, and understood, and gives him/her a sense of belonging, all of which are important factors of secure attachment. It helps him/her recognize you as someone safe with whom he/she can discuss challenging thoughts and ideas with, instead of turning to others for advice. Why is this so important? It's important because you are brain-building. You are helping your teen truly understand that he/she has everything needed inside of him/herself to figure tough things out if he/she asks the right questions and seeks the wisdom of the Holy Spirit. Your teen is learning how to think critically. You are training your teen to trust that the answer will come. It helps him/her be independent from the opinion of men and dependent on the Holy Spirit for guidance. You are training your teen to be able to help others use their minds and wait for God.

I hope you are seeing the difference in this kind of listening. It is relational and therefore the secret sauce to meaningful relationships. It is withness! By listening like this, you are training your teen's brain to be wave-rider listeners who hear God above all the other voices screaming for his/her attention. And it is a model of the relationship that Christ has with us.

## Withness Nugget:

When Jesus listened, He did not listen to criticize but to understand and engage at a deeper level with the participant. He listened to those who were hurting, to those who disagreed with Him, to those who wanted to harm Him, and to His enemies. He gave space for the recipient to receive the message and to consider it. Listening to understand will change all of your relationships, including the one with your young adult.

## Mindful Moments:

As you listen, tune in to yourself. What is happening internally for you? Notice if you are feeling safe or threatened. Is it more important for you to be right or to connect with your teen before you solve the problem together? Notice what happens for you internally when you challenge your thinking. Consider letting go of your need to be right all the time. What needs to happen now for you internally to regulate yourself to a place of safety and receptivity?

What makes you want to fight or run? What signals does your body send to warn you this experience is happening? What thoughts and feelings do you experience when you are in this sympathetic arousal state or survival mode?

## Journaling Reflections:

- Which listening style do you most resonate with?

- Which relationships bring out the best in your listening? The worst?

- For the ones that bring out the worst in your listening, who do you need to be to best connect with and affect that person?

# CHAPTER 24

# DEEP WATERS

---

Ever get taken out by a gigantic wave? Figuratively or literally, I'm sure we all have! I remember a time I was out in the ocean and there was a ledge that created a huge drop off. One minute I could stand, and the next I couldn't touch the bottom. It was at the moment I realized I couldn't stand anymore that an enormous wave came at me, pushing me under the water and spinning me around with reckless agitation. I lost my bearings, and there was an eerie silence as my open eyes watched all the movement below the surface. Heck, there was a lot going on under there! It was simultaneously beautiful and scary. I longed to get my feet on solid ground, but I had to stop fighting and let the deep waters have their way first. The minute I opened my eyes under water, I saw things from a different perspective. The waves that we see above the surface are not the only action; there is a lot going on under the surface as well. There is always a lot going on under the surface of the ocean, and the same is true for our teens.

We often look at the surface — at all the outward behaviors, attitudes, and actions — and then we react based on what we see. What if we changed our perspective for a moment and looked at what was going on under the surface?

What you see on the surface is a disrespectful tone. What may be going on under the surface is your teen was just rejected by her peer group and she is having huge emotions she doesn't know how to process. What you see on the surface is your son procrastinating doing his homework. What may be going on under the surface is he has a fear of failure.

Our busyness as parents often keeps us from looking under the surface. We think we don't have time to deal with the under-the-surface stuff or we're too busy to even consider that there could be under-the-surface stuff that needs to be addressed. In reality, this results in us spending as much if not more time fighting with and strong-arming our teens. There is a better way.

Our teens' brains are under construction. The prefrontal cortex (PFC), which handles higher executive functions, is still in the developmental stage. The PFC controls several key functions. The first function is the "braking center" of the brain. This part of the brain is fragile, temperamental, and energy hungry; it works best when you are not anxious, hungry, or tired. Using the PFC's veto power to manage impulses requires awareness, and the impulses have to be vetoed quickly for success, which requires practice. This is why your teen seems out of control sometimes, and it also explains why your teen loves high-risk activities and novelty. We can help them develop this function in their PFC; as a matter of fact, it's our job as parents.

Like the PFC, another part of the brain that is underdeveloped is the relational circuitry. I bet you can guess what this circuitry monitors: yup, emotions. This totally explains why teens are so moody!

As parents, we are "brain builders" (Siegel & Bryson, 2014). We help their brains develop — well or not so well — it's our choice. If we open our eyes and see what's going on under the surface, we're far more likely to help them develop well. So, will it be survival mode or thrive mode? When we function in survival mode — on cruise control — the circumstance triggers us and we react as if there is a threat. In thrive mode, we respond intentionally. This is where we pause, open our eyes, assess the situation, and respond thoughtfully, with brain-building at the front of our minds.

Part of teaching and disciping our teens has to do with receptivity. Our teens are not receptive to training that comes with lectures, mandates, and force. Receptivity comes when one brain connects with another brain. This feeling of connection creates the space for learning to take place. We need to connect with our teens in order to affect them. That is why withness as a witness is a powerful way to affect our teens and build their brains.

Every situation we encounter with our teens is an opportunity to form a connection so that we can affect them positively. "Interpersonal integration, the ability to honor differences between ourselves and others, and then connect through compassionate communication, empathy, and understanding another point of view, allows us to be different but connected to others. This integration in relationship creates integration in the brain of the neural pathways" (Siegel & Bryson, 2014, p.81). This is also why coaching is such a powerful tool for transformation. Coaching helps create neural connections and creates a safe place for others to be real and to explore possibilities. This connection with the coach helps facilitate lasting change in the client's brain. When we become coaches to our teens, we can respond as a loving and empowering guide instead of a helicopter parent.

A helicopter parent is a parent who jumps in to control, fix, and over-function to solve the teen's problem and shield his/her child from all difficulties and discomfort. He/She is someone who means well and wants so badly to help his/her teen solve the problem. What he/she doesn't realize is that this type of behavior actually disconnects him/her from his/her teen. It creates distance and disharmony. This is not brain-building; this is mom/dad using her/his brain to problem-solve. As teens pull away and develop their independence, this type of parenting often becomes frustrating to teens and actually keeps them stunted in their growth and development.

When you take a coach approach to parenting in difficult situations, you develop receptivity in your teen's brain by connecting with him/her. Once he/she is receptive, you can guide him/her to use — and therefore develop — his/her PFC by asking exploratory questions (developing curiosity) so that he/she can see the options available to him/her. This is a powerful parenting move! It's one that builds up instead of tears down. It's a move that helps him/her integrate his/her neural pathways so that he/she will get stronger and then be able to access those pathways when you are not around to assist him/her. This is a power move because it shows your teen that you believe in him/her, which deepens the connection between the two of you. It is withness as a witness and brain-building at its best!

I think it's important to pause here and say that connection in order to affect your teen does not mean agreement with all of his/her behaviors, responses, and actions. It does not mean taking a laissez-faire approach to parenting. It does not mean ignoring behavior. There will be instances you will need to have tough conversations with your teen and set boundaries. We will go into this later. However, those conversations will fall on deaf ears without connection. So connection, listening, and curiosity are the foundation to all important interactions with our teens if we desire to develop a deep and meaningful relationship of mutual respect with them.

When you keep the relationship at the forefront and focus on connection before you try to affect your teen, your teen will come to you and pick your brain during challenging times. He/She will not hide, because he/she will know you are safe. He/She will know that you are a brain-building parent who desires they become a fully integrated human who can use his/her whole brain, body, soul, mind, and strength.

## MANAGING THE RIPTIDES!

When exploring under the surface, you are bound to encounter riptides. Riptides are rapidly moving underwater currents caused by the tide. Riptides are strongest where flow is constricted. A swimmer may not realize the underwater current is changing and get swept away by a riptide. It is only by intentionally observing the changing tides that we can discover the forming riptide. When we are going about our time in the ocean on cruise control, we often miss the signs that the tide is shifting (which is how many newbie beachgoers drown). The same things happen in our households. We need to pay attention and be intentional to detect the signs of shifting tides, so that we can avoid being carried out to sea or drowning in a dangerous riptide!

When I was a young girl, we had this huge van. My dad was really into cars, and this was the new purchase he got for family vacations. It was fancy! We piled in the van with my aunt, uncle, and two cousins and started our journey to Florida. We were going to Daytona Beach, where we could drive on the sand with our fancy van and park and swim. The drive down from New Jersey seemed like it took forever! The cries of "are we there yet" echoed from the back of the van. We didn't have electronics back then, and my failing memory is that I can't remember what we did to entertain ourselves.

When we arrived, the parents lined up all four of their beach chairs in a row, and we all enjoyed the beach. While the rest of us kids were swimming in the ocean, my young cousin was floating on her raft. We were all having fun and didn't notice my cousin just floating away. Those on the shore thought she was with the rest of us kids, and we thought she was on the shore.

The fun was over. Panic set in for all of us.

We alerted the lifeguards, evacuated the waters, and searched for her. It was pretty dramatic. Thankfully, there is a happy ending. They found her a mile down shore and returned her to our family. Nowadays, the lifeguards are hyperaware of riptides and pay careful attention to the waters.

This story reminds me of many households where parents are like the untrained lifeguards watching the water when my cousin floated away — unconscious and unaware of the tides that are causing their teens to drift away. There's no need to continue parenting like this. In fact, it's dangerous to keep parenting like this. We don't have to just hope and pray the tide will correct itself and this impulsive, moody stage will pass. We can choose to be consciously aware of the changing tides and adapt to the pull. It requires intention and commitment to adopt a coach approach to parenting.

You need to engage with God and your teen to cooperate with God's work in your teen's heart. It's a conscious and deliberate effort. This work is messy, but it's satisfying to cooperate with the Spirit and your teen. This is the work of change and transformation that you get to take part in.

A common mistake that most people make when facing a riptide is that they fight against the tide. Anyone with experience in the sea knows that those that fight the riptide get tired, make mistakes, and often drown. The person who has experience with a riptide knows to allow the current to take you a bit out to sea, without a fight, and then shift to swim sideways to get out of the current. Just as initially riding the riptide and then shifting out of it is the easiest and safest way to escape it, initially riding with your teen's emotions in a time of stress (hearing and connecting) and then shifting to brain-building (coaching) empowers kids to see new possibilities out of the riptide.

You cannot help a drowning person caught in the riptide until he/she submits to your lead or rescue. Your teen needs to see you as a safe person with whom he/she can explore the options to escape the riptide he/she is in.

You cannot legislate faith — it is a supernatural work of the Spirit. But connection is a mandatory ingredient if you want to affect your kid's spiritual growth. This withness (connection with self, others, and God) is a bond that speaks volumes. I call it withness as a witness. Your message will be ignored and unheard if you react with a stress response, and your child's brain will shut down. Can God work without us? Yes, of course, but He delights to use us in the process of reaching our kids.

Our brains are wired to go toward someone in love or away from someone in fear. Strict legislation is an away, or fear, response. Teens will run for the hills and look for those who support the opposite of their parents if the house is ruled by a dictator. Even if parents are "right," teens are not going to hear them or respond inwardly to what they're saying. They may comply outwardly, but in the long run parents are losing their teen's heart.

Considering the brain's natural reaction to resistance, the shift for parents is thinking about what their teen is feeling instead of allowing yourself to feel it as much as (or sometimes even more than) your suffering teen.

So how do you incorporate this personally? Developing awareness of the energy and emotions that are flowing through your body will help keep you on track. When big emotions come to the surface, instead of diving in the deep end with your teen, it's best that you self-regulate. When you allow yourself to be carried away by your teen's big emotions, your nervous system becomes overloaded and you go into a fight, flight, freeze, or fawn mode. You cannot think clearly from a dysregulated state, because the brain sends all the oxygen to the large muscles so you can run for your life. You end up fighting the same riptide your teen is caught in. What if you chose differently? What if you self-regulated, and that stability became a source of strength for your teen?

My friend and colleague Pamela Mertz likes to use this visual (which she uses for coaching in general, but it applies here too): When you are coaching [your teen] on an emotionally charged topic that feels triggering for you, remember a time when he/she was a child and was ill and vomiting. You were there for support, and without [you holding] the bucket, it would have gotten messy.

Visualize this supportive bucket. See yourself in the caretaker role. You catch the vomit and you sit with your child. While you can't fix vomiting, you can still offer your presence for support. You touch his/her back, and you give space for his/her emotions, provide comfort, and are present with him/her. You remind yourself that you are not responsible for stopping the vomiting; that is and always will be outside your control. You are 100% responsible for your own emotions and responsible for being present and engaged with God and your child. Remind yourself that loving presence is a necessary ingredient to connect with him/her before you can affect him/her. You are present, self-regulated, and responsible for you and your emotions as you sit with your child in his/her big emotions. There is no work to be done besides holding the bucket to assist if needed — this is BEING!

You sit and you say little; maybe just small supportive comments, like "How can I best support you now?" Most times they will say, "Just listen" or "Be here." When the emotion or vomit stops, they might say, "Wow, thanks for being here." And you will think, "Really??? I did nothing." CORRECT ... YOU WERE JUST BEING PRESENT AND ENGAGED.

Similarly, your teen needs you to be in the game that is their life — not running the game, not refereeing the game, but a wise coach who gets curious and helps them find the answers that lie within. No one changes by being forced to change. No one changes when it's not their idea to change. This is how coaching helps empower others to step into their wisdom and connect with their God-given identity. I've said it before, and I'll say it again: In order to affect change, you must connect with that person. They must believe that you are "with" them and "for" them. They must believe you are on the same team and not a hostile adversary. This belief only occurs when you are present and walk in wholeness. Your teen can sense any misalignment between your words and actions. Your teen can differentiate between you promoting your own agenda and you encouraging creative thinking and problem-solving. Reacting to your teen's ideas and emotions with panic or outright rejection — instead of exploring curiously — can shut them down. Your teen is likely testing out new ideas, but they may not be certain about the connections yet. They are learning to establish their own identity apart from you and your beliefs. This is the normal growth and development pattern.

Many of us hear a thought come out of our teen's mouth and immediately go into lecture mode. We explain to them why their thoughts are incorrect, how the thoughts contradict their upbringing, or how their thoughts may be dangerous. What if you paused, took a few deep breaths, looked into their eyes, and connected? Imagine them at that moment as your five-year-old child. Tap into your relational circuitry, look at them with love, and get curious. Ask nonthreatening, open-ended questions. "Wow, that's a new thought. Tell me more about that." If you are engaged in your relational circuitry and self-regulated, you will not have a judgmental tone, body language, or attitude. Your words, being, and body will all match. You will authentically be curious, which allows you to go deeper into what is behind the thought that was brought up. This creates a safe place for your teen to explore their true identity. It also creates an environment of openness for when they have "big kid" problems they need to process. You must aspire to be a space of growth and grace for your family.

I have a personal example. One of my kids dropped a bomb on me at dinner one evening. Now, this is one of my better parenting moments; sadly, I've got hundreds of them I'm not proud of, but I share this one so you can see what it looks like when wave-rider listening plays out to completion.

One of my teens struggled with anxious and hypervigilant thinking. During dinner one night, she/he said, "My friends are smoking pot, and I'm thinking about doing it too." My nervous system immediately kicked into high gear and my heart raced. I felt my shoulders and jaw tighten as I clenched my teeth. In a split second my brain painted pictures for me, and I hated the pictures I was seeing. First, I saw my child sitting on his/her bed, disconnected from life. Next, my brain saw the random drug test that would rip the college scholarship away and that child returning to live in my basement for the rest of his/her life. If that wasn't enough, it then added the tragedy of him/her purchasing fentanyl-laced marijuana and ending up lying in a ditch. This is what the brain does when it detects danger. In the past, my reaction would have reflected the picture I just experienced in my mind, and I'd have overreacted with harshness to the statement.

Thankfully, I recognized the totally fear-based voice of the inner critic and invisible influencers trying to "help" me, and that I was dysregulating. I remembered that parenting based on fear leads to resistance, an endless tug of war, disconnection, withdrawal, and hiding. This kid was trying to figure out his/her way or he/she would not have mentioned it at the dinner table. He/She was a young adult and needed to make his/her own decisions. What he/she needed was a calm and regulated mom to hold space for him/her to think.

This time I showed up as my best self. I remember quickly silencing that inner voice and returning to the present. I took a deep breath to calm down and activate my ventral vagal system — I was able to regain my balance.

It's moments like these that the words of my mentor Cheryl Scanlan come to mind. She reminds us that in delicate situations where we feel ourselves reacting, we must remain like a duck — calm on the surface, yet paddling furiously under the surface to stay afloat and present. This is a classic word picture for me about self-regulating when triggered.

At that moment, I was able to shift out of survival mode and think clearly. My response was to lean in with a listening, nonjudgmental, open heart. I said little, but what I said brought me more time to think, listen, and "see" below the surface. My response was, "Wow. Tell me more about what you are thinking." Then I listened deeply to the new ideas they were processing with me. My teen was turning to me at this moment, not social media or anybody else. This was huge, especially given how strained our relationship used to be!

I listened without telling, without correcting, without judging, without an agenda. Most times, your young adult is just trying on a new identity. Their whole growth and development pattern is to belong with their peers and become an individual separate from you. Listen and learn. When we practice presence, we get to see below the surface as they drop valuable clues along the way. How we react sends our young adult messages of acceptance or rejection.

After I listened, understood, and validated where they were coming from, I said, "I can understand why you see it that way." I then asked, "Would you mind if I asked you a few more questions so you have all the facts as you make this big decision?" By doing this, I recognized their individuality and acknowledged their independent decision-making ability.

Now, moms, don't freak out here! We need to realize that they will make their own decisions when they are in college. By being curious and asking questions, I helped him/her develop his/her PFC, so that he/she would have the tools to make good decisions when I wasn't there. I also validated his/her trust in me as a safe person to bounce thoughts and ideas off of. If I had handled it the wrong way, I'd have slammed the door to communication — not just in the moment but also in the future.

Back to how I handled it. I asked him/her to list all the benefits of partaking. I did not discount their benefits, even though I wanted to, but I listened deeply. What I noticed was a theme. This child wanted to connect and belong. This was a normal part of a teen's growth and development; it was just coming in this "flavor" for my teen (for some, it might be purple hair or clothing that you don't care for).

I then had him/her list all the costs if he/she got caught doing what (at the time) was illegal. When he/she got to the college drug testing part, I took the questioning deeper.

Me: "What will happen if your spot check comes back positive?"
Son/Daughter: "I won't be able to play the sport I love."
Me: "What else?"
Son/Daughter: "I may lose my scholarship."
Me: "Then what?"

Son/Daughter: "I will have to go to community college and move back home for a while." (Disclaimer: There is no judgment regarding community college; it just wasn't a personal preference of said child.)

As we continued to explore, the list against partaking grew.

We used two mental lists to complete the discussion, which always helps slow down young adults from making impulsive decisions because of their underdeveloped PFC. This becomes your new role as a parent of a young adult. It is your role to get them to access their own braking system and slow down their decision-making. It's a shift from telling them what to think to helping them process their own thoughts with curious exploration.

I ended with the comment, "Great discussion. I believe you have everything you need to make a powerful decision. Let me know what you decide." By saying this, I acknowledged I didn't have control over his/her decision and that I BELIEVED he/she had everything he/she needed to make a wise choice for him/herself.

Now, my over-functioning mama's heart wanted to nag him/her every day to see what he/she decided. Each time I saw him/her, I had to resist the urge to ask. This was a success story of self-regulation for me — this time!

By taking this posture, it established a safe place for my teen to explore without judgment, without me pushing my agenda on him/her, and without me inducing shame, guilt, or anxiety. It gave him/her space to choose well. Now, some of you may be screaming right now, "I'm the parent, and while they are under my roof, they will submit to my rule." I say yes and no. There are certain boundaries that need to be established, but your young adult will make his/her own decisions while in college. Why not let your teen exercise his/her decision-making processes before leaving home?

Three weeks passed. My teen had forgotten the conversation, but I thought of nothing else. I had self-managed and resisted the urges to ask up to this point, but now the time was right to follow up. "Hey, what'd you decide about that pot thing?" "Oh, I decided it wasn't worth the risk." For me, this was a huge parenting win! This was a time of connection over control and love over fear, and it felt good to honor another human's space. It felt good to control what I could — my reaction to the inner turmoil I was experiencing. This was a win for me and for my young adult! No matter the outcome and what decision or subsequent action he/she took, which may or may not match this story, the win was for our relationship. The result: Our family was and is a safe place to explore hard things that differ from our values and beliefs. Leaders create win-win situations, and you are leaders, Mom and Dad.

Parenting well is about creating win-win situations where your young adult is capable and equipped to make his/her own best decisions daily. It's about helping him/her connect those decisions to the things that are most important to him/her, like values, dreams, and future goals. Micromanaging is a loss for all involved and is a game-over reaction. I've witnessed too many relationships that the grip of the control monster has forever fractured. Stop feeding the monster and start watering your love seeds. What you feed and water will grow. What fruit are you trying to produce?

You can change the way you interact with your young adult today. You can develop the fruit in your family that you've been secretly longing for. It all begins with you. You have more power than you know, and it begins within. As someone who has traveled this road imperfectly, I can help you access the inner tools you need to improve your relationships, increase love and respect in your household, and prepare your young adults to be the world changers that they dream to become. You are (or can be again) their main influencer — your voice and actions matter. It's time to stand up and let your love be heard.

 **Withness Nugget:**

Jesus asked lots of questions and then silently waited for others to process and decide. There was no controlling others' choices, decisions, and emotions. He was fully present with each person He contacted — without judgment and full of grace and truth. How can you be full of grace and truth with your teen without telling them, reprimanding them, judging them, or condemning them? How can you show up in unconditional love and grace today?

**Mindfulness Moments:**

Notice how your emotional and psychological states affect your family. Practicing co-regulation is our role with our teens. As stated above, your teen's brain is not fully developed so, they need to borrow some of our resources to soothe and manage their big emotions. Paying attention to the waves of emotion, without being carried away by it ourselves, provides our teens a stable base in which to co-regulate. By empathetically tuning in to our teens, we can help them modulate their emotions and return to the window of tolerance. What if you saw your teen as being just like you — in need of regulation? Can you be present without becoming overly charged and consumed with negative behaviors? Can you see your teen with the eyes of love, compassion, and grace?

How do we co-regulate with our teens? We begin with self-awareness and managing our own internal landscape by resourcing ourselves daily so that we can provide a safe space for our teens to show up as is. We get to show up calm, clear, focused, and courageously as we sit with them in their big emotions from a place of empathetic curiosity. When you show up this way, your teen knows they are safe, seen, soothed, and secure to be themselves and still be loved. They will catch your stable emotions and regulation through their mirror neurons and begin to co-regulate with you; they will also learn how to reset and self-regulate.

The reverse is also true. When we shift out of the window of tolerance with our dysregulated teen, this is also contagious.

Notice these things today.

 **Journaling Reflections:**

- What have you noticed triggers you into a reactive state with your teen?

- How can you prepare ahead of time and bypass the dysregulation in the moment?

- What practices can you put in place to be sure you are resourced when your teen is not?

- How might you shift from yelling and telling your teen to demonstrating, modeling, and asking curious questions? Create one practical next step to practice.

## CHAPTER 25

# DECISION FATIGUE AND THE BRAIN

---

Decisions, decisions, decisions ... it seems like our brains are bombarded with decisions! According to an article in Psychology Today (2018), the average person makes around 35,000 decisions a day — unless you are a working mom, then I would double that (that's just Doreen guessology 😊 ). Heck, a study by Cornell University revealed that we make 226.7 daily decisions about food alone (Oberbrunner, 2021). This doesn't even take into account the constant questions from kids and your parenting responsibilities! Does anyone else feel stressed out as you see how much your brain is juggling? You are not alone!

The more decisions you have to make, the more fatigued your brain becomes. Our brain only has a certain amount of energy each day, and when we have used it all up, our decisions get worse and we make mistakes. With mistakes comes stress, and stress amplifies poor decision-making. The effects of this chronic, draining cycle are fatigue and brain fog!

Stress leads to dysregulation, and dysregulation can lead to Route Survive, and Route Survive often leads you to make poor decisions. When on Route Survive, our bodies work hard to conserve energy, shifting all the oxygen away from the PFC. Translation: You get reactive — fight, flight, freeze, or fawn.

Fatigued brains take the path of least resistance — the superhighways through the survive region. But it doesn't have to be this way. We can choose how we interpret and process the stimuli we have to process. We get to choose what we give our energy to daily!

Daily bombardment by constant stimuli has become inescapable. We need to be intentional about guarding our internal landscape. Daily we face decisions that either move us toward our goals, our desired relationships, and to a place of withness — or they move us away from these things. So are you multitasking or switch-tasking? Are you wasting energy listening to the inner critic and his gang, or are you letting the wisdom keep you grounded and in your window of tolerance? You get to choose the stimuli that takes up space in your brain. It's a choice.

There is a goal I have been working at for the past 15 years — each year I've been growing, learning, and improving, growing closer and closer to reaching it. I was really close one day — the goal was totally within reach. But then I had one too many decisions to make and my goal was delayed indefinitely. But I now recognize the delay as a gift and opportunity because I learned another great lesson for my life's journey. Mastering self-regulation is the key to reaching this goal; but, win or lose, functioning from a space of self-regulation and withness with God, others, and myself is more important. This life journey has been a process, sometimes facing a fixed mindset and other times living out of a growth mindset.

Achieving this goal will not change my life in any significant way — but the "trophy" will represent massive growth in self-regulation and withness as a witness to His presence within me. As I've progressed toward attaining my goal, it's been messy — but isn't that how God likes it? I'm reminded of 2 Corinthians 12:9-11 in the middle of my messiness: "But he said to me, 'My grace is sufficient for you, for my power is made perfect in weakness.' Therefore, I will boast all the more gladly about my weaknesses, so that Christ's power may rest on me. This is why, for Christ's sake, I delight in weaknesses, in insults, in hardships, in persecutions, in difficulties. For when I am weak, then I am strong."

I was so close to reaching my goal, when suddenly, it happened. I looked away. I got tired; I had decision fatigue. God had me right where He wanted me — in total dependence on Him (Matthew 26:40-41). But 10 minutes from reaching my goal, I turned toward man instead of God — and it cost me the goal. I momentarily took my eyes off my power source, and I sank (Matthew 14:22-23). In decision fatigue, I reacted instead of responding.

Fatigue is to be expected, and failure is inevitable — but the great thing is, we get to grow through it all.

The mistake was returning to old patterns of problem-solving on Route Survive instead of remaining on Route Thrive in withness with THE ultimate power source. I'm reminded of someone else who turned back to his old patterns of problem-solving. Peter, after multiple failures, quit following Jesus and went back to fishing (John 21:3). He didn't stay fishing for long because God had bigger plans for his life — and He has bigger plans for yours as well. Even when you don't see them, you can trust that "fishing" is not the end goal for you.

It's tempting to run and hide when life goes off the rails, but that is just fear-based living rearing its ugly head! We were created for more. We were created to love, connect, and affect. Are you willing to live a life of love over a life of fear? It all starts with you, because self-regulation mastery is one of the keys to happiness and success, and it's done in connection with God, others, and self when you choose love pathways over fear pathways — it is walking in wholeness. This is withness as a witness to His great and abundant love.

"There is no fear in love, but perfect love casts out fear." — 1 John 4:18 (ESV)

 **Stillness and Silence**

In the world of busyness, constant stimuli, distraction, and disconnection — silence and stillness are life-giving.

Practice stillness and silence: no podcasts, no music, no sound — just silence. You may be uncomfortable with silence — stick with it and notice what happens in your body and mind. Keep breathing through the discomfort of the silence, for this is where the nuggets lie.

It is in this stillness that we get to hear God's voice, think deeply, and reflect on our next best steps. Begin with some deep breaths. Remove any distractions — shut down the phone and the computer, and maybe even get into nature.

As you begin this, you may want to start with 5 minutes and increase as you progress in your practice. "Be still and know that I am God" (Psalm 46:10).

Approach this time with the excitement of being WITH yourself and God — it's like personal time with your best friend and perfect wisdom. God had the prescription before anyone else: "In quietness and trust is your strength" (Isaiah 30:15).

# GLOSSARY

**Anxiety:** Emotional feelings and sensations of fear or impending doom. It is the hyperarousal of the sympathetic nervous system and downregulation of the social engagement system and ventral vagal circuit.

**Attachment:** An emotional bond developed by two individuals, such as a parent and child. When the attachment is secure, the child feels safe, seen, soothed, and secure. There is secure and several types of insecure attachment that affect behavior and patterns in adulthood. These patterns can be rewired and addressed. "Attachment develops through joy and the idea that you are glad to be with someone." — Dr. Allan Schore (Wilder (quoting a conversation with Schore), 2020, p. 76)

**Attunement:** An appropriate tuning in to another person's emotional needs and responding with appropriate language and behaviors of support and trustworthiness. It is the ability to detect and sense what might be happening under the surface for another.

**Autonomic Nervous System:** This is the system that keeps you safe and alive, which works subconsciously. It includes the sympathetic nervous system and the parasympathetic nervous system, which has two branches — the ventral vagus and the dorsal vagus circuits.

**Breathing:** Breathing is your life force to deliver oxygen to the brain, organs, and body. Deep breathing activates the parasympathetic nervous system through the vagus nerve. This activation regulates the sympathetic nervous system's fight and flight responses, which in turn allows us to self- and co-regulate, so we can think clearly and behave like ourself again.

**Capacity:** One's ability to manage internal and external stimuli and remain charged, bounce back quickly to stability, and be flexible. When your capacity is diminished, you can become dysregulated.

**Circuitry:** These are the neural pathways in your brain that electrical and chemical signals travel. Siegel states, "Neurons that fire together wire together" (Siegel & Bryson, 2014, p. 42) This circuitry is shaped biologically (genes) and by the experiences we have had. There are circuits that shape or support different behavior. These circuits are triggered by stimuli from inside and outside the body. The more one uses a specific circuitry, the more easily and frequently that circuitry is chosen for processing stimuli.

**Cognitive Load:** The amount of information we are trying to hold in our brain at one time. When in multisensory overload, our energy is drained.

**Coping Mechanisms:** Skills used to intentionally manage stressful situations.

**Co-regulation:** Moments of safe connection with others, which has a calming effect. We were made to connect and affect, which are needed for survival. One needs to feel safe with another in order to co-regulate.

**Cranial Nerves:** Nerves that come from the brain and spinal cord and deliver motor and sensory stimuli to the brain. There are 12 pairs of cranial nerves.

**Deep Rest:** Restorative and regenerative rest, which comes through meditation, silence, heart breathing, nervous system relaxation techniques, and the deep sleep phase (where special cells in your brain called the clean-up crew remove debris).

**Defense Mechanisms:** Automatic and subconscious reactions to stressful situations. Defense mechanisms are negative ways we deal with stress and are often the result of trauma, lack of learned skills, or lack of self-awareness. See stress patterns.

**Demands:** External and internal stimuli that compete for your attention and drain your resources and energy. Also known as stress.

**Dissociation:** Disconnection from the present during a threat reaction. It is an adaptive reaction by which a person keeps him/herself safe during trauma or overwhelming circumstances by internally disconnecting from the event. Also known as "checking out."

**Distractors:** A distractor is an action we take, subconsciously, when we feel an uncomfortable emotion arising. It is a technique we turn to so that we can feel better. You may notice a sensation in your body during a scary movie and reach for your phone as a distractor. This act actually pushes the feeling of fear into the body, without processing it. You could feel embarrassed and you laugh or roll your eyes. Distractors are also known as defenses.

**Dorsal Vagal Branch:** The backside of the vagus nerve in the parasympathetic nervous system. When activated, it moves us away from connection and into protection — shutting down the system during the freeze or faint cycle of the hypoarousal state in the window of tolerance. It is a low-energy state that can lead one to dissociation. A person feels like they are just going through the motions of life without caring, leading to depression and physical symptoms.

**Dysregulated:** The inability to control and/or manage one's emotions and behaviors or react intentionally in response to a threat, either real or perceived. Dysregulation occurs when one leaves the window of tolerance and enters a fight, flight, freeze, or faint reaction. In this state, the stimuli and emotions appear much bigger and out of control. Dysregulation is ruled by the fear circuitry in the brain and is a way your brain and body work together to keep you safe from a real or perceived threat. It is when a stressor's demands exceed the resources to manage them.

**Embodied Self-Awareness:** A whole-body awareness that incorporates interoception, exteroception, and proprioception. These somatic processing abilities allow us to be in the present moment. Sensations can only be experienced in the present moment.

**Emotional Contagion:** Emotions and/or behavior that spread like wildfire in a group.

**Epigenetics:** The study of how behavior and environment can affect the way your body reads your DNA sequence on a molecular level.

**Episodic Memory:** The bridge between the unconscious and the explicit memory, which helps us make sense of our memories and build coherent narratives. The two subcategories of this memory are emotional memories and procedural memories.

**Essence:** The essence of a human is the unique makeup of mind, will, soul, spirit, and creative capacity that is distinct to the person. Each human is uniquely wired in the mother's womb by God, making us different from other animals in the animal kingdom — we were created in His image. Many times the essence of who we were created to be gets distorted by life's circumstances and our thoughts and beliefs. Most of life is a journey back to our true identity and connection with God.

**Explicit Memory:** A memory that we actually remember in our cognitive mind (e.g., studying for a test). These memories are stored in the hippocampus (filing cabinet). Over time, some of those "files" get lost or mislabeled, depending on the circumstance on how it's stored. These memories aren't always kept forever unless the memories have certain emotional charges with them.

**Exteroception:** One's ability to sense, perceive, and receive stimuli from outside the body. This stimuli enters through the senses.

**FACES:** An acronym by Dr. Daniel Siegel for F-flexible, A-adaptive, C-coherent, E-energized, and S-stable.

**Fast-Track System:** This is the automatic, high-speed pathway that reminds us of who we are and how we belong, before conscious thought occurs. It helps us trust, predict, appreciate, calm oneself, dictate social and moral behavior, and connect with our values and identity. A well-trained fast track leads to mental shortcuts or habits that help us filter information to the prefrontal cortex (PFC). This fast-track system travels at 6 cycles per second, whereas the slow track travels at 5 cycles per second. This tells us that conscious thought happens after automatic fast-track relational skills. When the fast track completes its cycle and is fueled by joy, your relational capacities and psychological safety skyrocket. When it does not complete its cycle — it goes offline. The fast track can be developed. When information travels the fast track to the prefrontal cortex (PFC), the PFC can then filter and assign tasks and problems to the slow-track system.

**Felt Sense:** Subconscious feeling or full-body perception through internal and external sensations. It is an inner body "knowing" — aka our "gut" or "sixth sense." It's a process of noticing sensations, such as butterflies in the stomach, and then listening to what those sensations are trying to communicate.

**Fixed Mindset:** The inability to see challenges and setbacks through the lens of possibility and learning. A fixed mindset occurs from fear-based thinking and the accompanying negativity bias and limiting beliefs that keep a person stuck in maladaptive patterns.

**Growth Mindset:** The ability to see challenges and setbacks through the lens of possibility and learning.

**Heart Coherence:** A state of wellness when our body's systems are in sync and harmonious. The heart sends more messages to the brain than the brain sends to the heart. It is an order and harmony created in the mental, emotional, and bodily processes where the two autonomic nervous system branches (sympathetic and parasympathetic) are in sync, creating internal balance. This can be measured by heart rate variability, blood pressure, and respiratory rate. When we are in a coherent state we are calm, confident, clear, and focused; we are our best selves in an open-hearted state. Negative emotions contribute to a lack of coherence, and positive emotions/appreciation contribute to coherence.

**Holy Noticing:** Noticing God's presence through mutual mind in the space between one's circumstance and their subsequent reaction/response. This is a space of pause, oneness, and connection that is a felt sense. It is experiential comfort, wisdom, grace, mercy, and the supernatural presence of God working in and through us. It is a deep spiritual connection to self, others, and God and His creation that is accessed through the relational circuitry in the brain.

**Hyperarousal:** This is the high-energy, automatic reaction by the sympathetic nervous system to a real or perceived threat. Also known as fight and flight, one has difficulty calming down and is chaotic. This is the brain–body accelerator, or gas pedal.

**Hypoarousal:** This is a low-energy, automatic reaction by the dorsal vagal branch of the parasympathetic nervous system in response to a real or perceived threat. It represents rigidity, freezing, numbness, and checked out characteristics and results in freeze or faint reactions and possible dissociation — this is the brain–body braking system.

**Identity:** A sense of who you are in your being as an individual and as a member in your social group at the essence level. When you disengage from the social engagement system, you no longer act like yourself and begin to react from the fear-based portion of your brain, as demonstrated by your stress patterns of choice.

**Implicit Memory:** A memory that lives in your body and subconscious as a felt sense. Think brushing your teeth, riding a bike, or driving a car; once you learn these things, you no longer need to consciously recall how to do them from your memory. This memory system is connected to the survive circuitry and looks for threats and safety cues. Emotionally charged memories can become fixed (e.g., flashbacks). When we put words to the sensations in an implicit memory, it is called "implicit narrative."

**Interoception:** The ability to sense, feel, perceive, label, and notice what is happening inside one's body.

**Integration:** When the different parts of a system work harmoniously together (through synaptic connections).

**Judge:** An internal voice that fixates on the negative in people, places, and things. It revolves around fear, frustration, failure, shame, blame, and condemnation. This is the main internal voice that beats a person up for real and perceived shortcomings.

**Linkage:** Different parts of the brain that are linked together by synaptic connections, allowing these parts to work together with flexibility and adaptability (see FACES above), leading to integration. When neurons in the brain fire together, they become linked, forming patterns in the brain.

**Mindful:** Awareness in the present moment.

**Mindsight:** Mindsight is the ability to focus one's attention on the inner world — thoughts and feelings — of self and others. We are able to tap into the relational circuitry and "see" the mind of the person in front of us. We can sync with others, or attune to them, in this state of being. It is sensing the internal and external, having insight and then inner compassion for yourself and another.

**Mutual Mind:** Mutual mind develops in a mindful state and connects a person mind-to-mind with another. Here a person can tap into the deeper wisdom and guidance of God. It can be communication without words that takes place from the fast-track system. Wilder uses passing a ball while running as an example. It requires sensing the other person's speed and direction and fully coordinating our actions with the one we are passing the ball to (2020).

**Neuroception:** Your nervous system's notification system that tells you if something or someone is dangerous or safe. It is your internal instincts, or intuition. This is the part of the nervous system that we often ignore only to regret it later.

**Neuroplasticity:** The brain's ability to make new connections (form new synapses), or pave new pathways. This occurs at an epigenetic level.

**Numbing:** Actions taken to stop emotional pain and the pain's repercussions using maladaptive substitutes (e.g., alcohol, excessive eating); these substitutes only temporarily block the emotions.

**Overthinking:** The act of thinking about something in a circular manner, including ruminating. This comes from overactive fear circuitry, a fixed mindset, and sometimes faulty perceptions, thoughts, and beliefs.

**Pause:** When we pause in that micro-second between the fast and slow tracks.

**Perception:** The ability to see, hear, or become aware of something through the senses by intuitive recognition, appreciation, understanding, or the interpretation of external or internal stimuli.

**Polyvagal Theory:** The concept (rediscovered by Stephen Porges) that there are "two vagal pathways in the nervous system that regulate the heart and heart–face connection to communicate what is happening inside our bodies to other people" (Dana, 2021, p. 5). There are two circuits (ventral vagal and the dorsal vagal), and three pathways of the autonomic nervous system lead to these circuits. The right vagus nerve connects to the heart and the braking system; information flows two ways in this pathway (80% of the information travels from the body to the brain and 20% from the brain to the body). If a person is disconnected from their body, the ability to tune in to information is lost. Porges found that there are three main principles that the body uses to address rest, breathing, digestion, and heart rate. The stimuli travels through the vagal nerve, which begins in the brainstem, and travels to many of the body's organs.

**Positive Intelligence:** A framework (by Shirzad Chamine) that combines research in factor analysis of neuroscience, positive psychology, performance science, and cognitive behavioral science. This framework addresses the root factors that empower one to build new neural pathways in the brain to improve wellness, stress management, relationships, leadership, and performance.

**Positive Stress:** Regular physiological stress that has a positive effect on our well-being and develops resilience. Your brain needs just the right amount of stress to function optimally — anything less, boredom occurs — anything more, it becomes negative stress. Also known as challenge stress.

**Predictions:** Your brain is a predicting machine and makes predictions to determine if something is a threat or reward. Safety is the goal of these predictions based on needs and requirements for survival. These predictions are best guesses by your brain based on memories that have been logged via previous experience. These predictions are faulty when data is mislabeled, misread, or misunderstood. Your expectations shape your perceptions and beliefs, and then your brain will look for evidence to prove you correct.

**Presence:** Conscious awareness of the current moment while looking toward the possibilities through eyes of love instead of eyes of fear and threat. This is done through deep listening and curiosity, which enables connection to others, self, and God. This is when others experience a felt sense of being seen, heard, and understood when they are WITH you.

**Proprioception:** The ability to sense where you are in space. It includes balance and relies heavily on input from the inner ear.

**Relational Circuitry:** The neural pathways where executive functioning is accessed, enabling intentionality and responsiveness. When stimuli is processed in these pathways, a person can connect with self, others, and God and view circumstances as possibilities, opportunities, and gifts.

**Resilience:** The ability to bounce back quickly from life's challenges with a growth mindset.

**Resonance:** When the mirror neurons respond to surrounding emotions and behaviors in alignment with another. This resonance can be negative or positive. See emotional contagion and attunement.

**Resourced:** When you are living mindfully and intentionally from a self-regulated space within the window of tolerance. You are able to manage the daily stressors effectively without dysregulation, disconnection, or self-abandonment.

**Saboteurs:** These are the internal influencers that automatically kick in when facing challenging circumstances. They can trigger a chain of thoughts, feelings, and actions in your mind, most times from a fixed mindset and carry with them negative feelings and judgments about people, places, and things. Saboteurs run in specific and identifiable patterns of behavior that interfere with your happiness. Saboteurs were developed in childhood to survive real or imagined threats, developing into your go-to patterns when threatened. These saboteurs helped you in the past, but they never contribute to happiness. Saboteurs can be disrupted.

**Sage Perspective:** A perspective that sees the possibilities, gifts, and opportunities in any situation. This perspective does not deny, reject, or resent what is but accepts reality, looking at it through eyes of love instead of fear.

**Safety:** A belief that you will not be punished, shamed, or ridiculed for showing up in your identity and for voicing your beliefs, concerns, or questions. When the brain's neuroception system flags potential threats, you access the fear circuitry instead of the relational circuitry, and the brain goes into protection mode. Intimacy cannot be established in an unsafe relationship or environment.

**SCARF:** A model of human social experience (coined by David Rock) describing threat and reward domains in the brain that either draw us toward or push us away from something. These five domains are:

<u>S</u>tatus: a sense of personal worth

<u>C</u>ertainty: a sense of what the future holds

<u>A</u>utonomy: a sense of control over one's life

<u>R</u>elatedness: a sense of safety with others

<u>F</u>airness: a sense of impartiality

**Self-Awareness:** Awareness of all aspects of time — past, present, and future. This awareness puts language, facts, and interpretations with incoming stimuli — shining a light on the thoughts, feelings, motives, and desires.

**Self-Regulation:** One's ability to assess, monitor, evaluate, and manage your energy — emotions, behaviors, responses and reactions to stimuli — from the internal and external worlds without any aid from another person. It includes noticing the real or perceived threats that come in the form of stimuli and then calming, quieting, and responding intentionally from a resourced space. Self-regulation allows you to act like yourself and return to joy quickly, living harmoniously with others, self, and God.

**Sensory Feedback Systems:** Interoception, exteroception, and proprioception are part of sensory feedback loops that are the core to embodied self-awareness.

**Slow-Track System:** When the slow-track system works without the fast-track completing its cycle and delegating to it, the slow track resorts to shame, blame, fear, and low psychological safety — resorting to predator or bully-like behavior. This puts the problem above the relationship. These are the clues that our fast-track system is offline. When stimuli is first filtered through the fast-track system (relational circuitry), creativity, curiosity, innovation, and learning occur. The prefrontal cortex can then use the slow-track's positive features (being rational, deliberate) for problem-solving. It allows us to direct our attention and make good and wise decisions.

**Social Engagement System:** This system has five circuits that connect with the ventral vagal branch of the parasympathetic system that controls our eyes, ears, and voice, the way we move our head, and the heart–face connection. This is how we scan faces and hear sounds that notify us whether we are safe or in danger.

**Somatic Nervous System:** This system monitors 1) sensory input (sound, smell, taste, and touch, but not sight) and 2) the sensations that control movement or your body's position in space. This sensory information travels through the vagus nerve and communicates and integrates all the information from the cranial nerves. It has to do with interoception, exteroception, proprioception, and neuroception.

**Stress Patterns:** Your go-to patterns of behavior when entering a dysregulated state. These are developed to keep you safe. These patterns can turn into habits that occur subconsciously. These patterns of behavior jump into action based on the reward system. For instance, if your brain has learned that being a people pleaser generates love, your brain will see that behavior as a go-to pattern. This can show up as any of your saboteurs, distractors, or defense mechanisms. The brain categorizes behaviors based on reward or threat; sometimes these behaviors are mislabeled as good for us, when they are not. See defense mechanisms.

**Stress Resilience** The ability to handle stressors without entering dysregulation. By creating opportunities that stretch our comfort zone, we can increase our capacity for handling stress. Techniques for increasing stress resilience include HIIT (high-intensity interval training), breath work, cold water therapy (5-10 seconds of full-body cold water exposure; it won't be comfortable, but it is not actually causing damage), and sauna therapy (core temperature increases for no more than 30 minutes (may need to build up to 30 minutes).

**Survival Mode:** Dysregulation of the nervous system that automatically activates self-criticism and condemnation — aka the Judge and the saboteurs. Self-criticism and condemnation cause us to lose the ability for self-compassion. Negative emotions, limiting beliefs, and a fixed mindset are the result.

**Sympathetic Nervous System:** This system is responsible for pumping blood to the body and managing heart rhythm and breathing patterns. When this system is balanced by the ventral vagal braking system, all is well. This branch is in charge of the fight and flight patterns of reaction to threat (real or perceived). When that braking system goes offline, connection with other people is lost and they may feel like enemies, and there is often a sense of impending doom. Hypervigilance is common in this dysregulated state, resulting in misreading cues and tones of voice.

**Thrive Region:** Ventral vagal regulation or the window of tolerance. In this space we are calm, courageous, curious, focused, connected, and joyful. We experience positive emotions, have a growth mindset, and can see possibilities.

**Transformation:** The experience of integration and wholeness, where the separate parts of us function from a place of wellness and love instead of a place of threat and fear.

**Trauma:** There are big-T traumas (threats of death, serious illness, and sexual violence) and little-t traumas (bullying, loss of a relationship; emotional abuse, harassment, death of a pet). The difference between them is described as "too much too soon" (a deeply disturbing or life-threatening event) or "too little for too long" (long-term exposure to distressing but not life-threatening events). When these experiences are not processed completely via your nervous system, the trauma is logged in the body. Left unprocessed, your body will manifest disease. One's body can only run in survival mode for so long before it begins to shut down; this is why stress patterns are not meant to be long-term solutions for your stress.

**Trust:** The experience of safety with another person that allows vulnerability, reliance, and confidence that they will not hurt you.

**Vagal Brake:** This inhibitory influence affects the heart's internal pacemaker, decreasing the heart rate.

**Ventral Vagal Branch:** This branch of the parasympathetic nervous system allows us to connect, communicate, and feel safe with another when not under threat situations. Dana states, "When the ventral vagal branch is activated, we acknowledge the 'distress, explore options, [and] reach out for and offer support" (2021, p.17). From this branch we are resourced, resourceful, joyful, playful, focused, present, and connected. Think window of tolerance — in the window is where we are able to develop self-compassion.

**VUCA:** This acronym — which stands for volatile, uncertain, complex, and ambiguous — has been thrown around about the society we are living in right now.

**Window of Tolerance:** A term (coined by Dr. Daniel Siegel) for the optimal state of arousal to function in a space of thriving instead of surviving. In the window of tolerance, one can notice, manage, regulate, and function from a space of focus, harmony, and calmness. When a client has experienced trauma (big T or little t), the window of tolerance is narrow and the person can easily be thrown out of balance and into dysregulation. The good news is this window of tolerance can be expanded and developed.

# REFERENCES

Ackerman, C. E. (2018, April 27). *What is attachment theory? Bowlby's 4 stages explained*. Original source unknown. Posted on PositivePsychology.com. (2023, April 19). https://positivepsychology.com/attachment-theory/#:~:text=Examples%3A%20The%20Types%2C%20Styles%2C,Avoidant%2C%20Ambivalent%2C%20and%20Disorganized

Amen, D. G. (2020, September 16). *Do you have an ANT infestation in your head*? Amen Clinics. https://www.amenclinics.com/blog/do-you-have-an-ant-infestation-in-your-head/

American Institute of Stress. (n.d.). *What is stress?* https://www.stress.org/daily-life

Barbash, E. (2017, March 13). *Different types of trauma: small 't' versus large 'T'*. Psychology Today. https://www.psychologytoday.com/us/blog/trauma-and-hope/201703/different-types-trauma-small-t-versus-large-t

Blake, A. (2018). *Your body is your brain: Leverage your somatic intelligence to find purpose, build resilience, deepen relationships and lead more powerfully*. Embright.

Betz, A. (n.d.). *The Orchestra of Your Brain* [Blog]. Beabove. https://www.beaboveleadership.com/2019/07/12/the-orchestra-of-your-brain/

Boehman, S. (n.d.). *Vulnerability hangover* [Podcast]. Make Money as a Life Coach, Episode 45. https://staceyboehman.com/vulnerability-hangover/

Boyatzis, R., Smith, M. L., & Van Oosten, E. (2019). *Helping people change: Coaching with compassion for lifelong learning and growth*. Harvard Business Review Press.

Brown, B. (2015). *Daring greatly: How the courage to be vulnerable transforms the way we live, love, parent, and lead.* Avery.

Brown, B. (2022). *The gifts of imperfection.* Hazelden Publishing.

Chamine, S. (2012). *Positive intelligence: Why only 20% of teams and individuals achieve their true potential and how you can achieve yours.* Greenleaf Book Group Press.

Chamine, S., & Barnhart, M. (2022). *Research foundation for positive intelligence assessments.* Positive Intelligence Whitepaper Series. https://www.positiveintelligence.com/wp-content/uploads/2022/07/Whitepaper-Research-Foundation-for-Positive-Intelligence-Assessments.pdf

Clear, J. (2018). *Atomic habits: An easy & proven way to build good habits & break bad ones.* Avery.

Collins, G. (2009). *Christian Coaching: Helping Others Turn Potential into Reality (2nd Ed.).* Navpress.

Coursey, C. M. (2021). *The joy switch: How your brain's secret circuit affects your relationships – and how you can activate it.* Northfield Publishing.

Covey, S. (2020). *7 habits of highly effective people.* Simon & Schuster.

Dana, D. (2021). *Anchored: How to befriend your nervous system using polyvagal theory.* Sounds True.

Dana, D. (2023). *Polyvagal practices: Anchoring the self in safety.* W. W. Norton & Company.

Duhigg, C. (2014). *The power of habit: Why we do what we do in life and business.* Random House.

Epel, E. (2022). *The stress prescription: Seven days to more joy and ease.* Penguin Life.

Fosha, D., Siegel, D. J., & Solomon, M. F. (Eds.). (2009). *The healing power of emotion: Affective neuroscience, development & clinical practice.* W. W. Norton & Company.

Frey, S. (2022). *The neuroscience of positive intelligence.* Positive Intelligence Whitepaper Series. https://www.positiveintelligence.com/wp-content/uploads/2022/05/neuroscience-of-positive-intelligence-2022-v1-0.pdf

Get Back to Life. (2010, January 28). *Stages of Emotional Liberation.* https://www.getbacktolife.org/blog/2017/11/29/stages-of-emotional-liberation

Hallam, R. (May 2023). *From clever to wise: How healing ourselves heals the world.* Freedom Summit for Medical Professionals: Expert Secrets to Navigate Stress, Beat Exhaustion, and Focus on What Matters.

Hendel, H. J. (2018). *It's not always depression: Working the change triangle to listen to the body, discover core emotions, and connect to your authentic self.* Random House.

Hull, M. (Ed.) (2023, August 24). *Mental health disorders.* The Recovery Village. https://www.therecoveryvillage.com/mental-health/

Jarfari, S. (2022, September 25). *Three stages from emotional slavery to emotional liberation.* LinkedIn. https://www.linkedin.com/pulse/three-stages-from-emotional-slavery-liberation-sharib-jafari/

Johnson, K. A. (2021). *Call of the wild: How we heal trauma, awaken our own power, and use it for good.* Harper Wave.

Kahneman, D. (2013). *Thinking, fast and slow.* Farrar, Straus and Giroux.

Katie, B. (n.d.). *The work is a practice* [Exercise]. The Work of Byron Katie. https://thework.com/instruction-the-work-byron-katie/

Keller, T. (2019, March 30). @timkellernyc. [Tweet]. X (formerly known as Twitter). https://twitter.com/timkellernyc/status/1112014190221377536

Kilner, J. M., & Lemon, R. N. (2013). What we currently know about mirror neurons. *Current Biology : CB, 23*(23), R1057–R1062. https://doi.org/10.1016/j.cub.2013.10.051

Kornfield, J., & Siegel, D. J. (2010). *Mindfulness and the brain: A professional training in the science and practice of meditative awareness.* Sounds True.

Krockow, E. M. (2018). How many decisions do we make each day. Psychology Today.

Lehman, A. (n.d.). *Big T vs little t trauma.* Grief Recovery Center. https://www.griefrecoveryhouston.com/big-t-vs-little-t-trauma/

Levine, P. (2008). *Healing trauma: A pioneering program for restoring the wisdom of your body.* Sounds True.

Levine, P. A. (1997). *Waking the tiger: Healing trauma.* North Atlantic Books.

Levine, P. A. (2015). *Trauma and memory: Brain and body in a search for the living past.* North Atlantic Books.

Maslach, C., & Leiter, M. P. (2022). *The burnout challenge: Managing people's relationships with their jobs*. Harvard University Press.

Merriam-Webster. (2023). *Merriam-Webster Unabridged Collegiate Dictionary*. Britannica Digital Learning. https://unabridged.merriam-webster.com/collegiate/attunement

Mind Tools Content Team. (n.d.). *David Rock's SCARF Model*. https://www.mindtools.com/akswgc0/david-rocks-scarf-model

Oberbrunner, K. (2021). *Unhackable: The elixir for creating flawless ideas, leveraging superhuman focus, and achieving optimal human performance*. Ethos Collective.

Oberbrunner, K. (n.d.). *Are you getting hacked?* [Video]. https://unhackablebook.com/

Porges, S. W. (2017). *The pocket guide to polyvagal theory: The transformative power of feeling safe*. W. W. Norton & Company.

Porges, S. W. (2023). *What's happening in the nervous system of patients who "please and appease" (or fawn) in response to trauma?* [Video]. National Institute for the Clinical Application of Behavioral Medicine. https://www.nicabm.com/working-with-please-and-appease/

Robbins, T. (2022, June 13). *@TonyRobbins* [Tweet]. X (formerly known as Twitter). https://twitter.com/TonyRobbins/status/1536370847555809281?lang=en

Rock. R. (2020). *Your brain at work: Strategies for overcoming distraction, regaining focus, and working smarter all day long*. Harper Business.

Rosenberg, M. (2015). *Nonviolent communication: A language of life*. PuddleDancer Press.

Ross, C. A. (2018, April 30). Talking about God with trauma survivors. *American Journal of Psychotherapy, 70*(4), 429–437. https://doi.org/10.1176/appi.psychotherapy.2016.70.4.429

Rothschild, B. (2000). *The body remembers: The psychophysiology of trauma and trauma treatment*. W. W. Norton & Company.

Siegel, D. J. (n.d.). *Comprehensive interpersonal neurobiology* [Course]. Mindsight Institute. https://mindsightinstitute.com/product/the-mindsight-approach-to-well-being-a-comprehensive-course-in-interpersonal-neurobiology/

Siegel, D. J. (2010). *Mindsight: The new science of personal transformation*. Bantam Books.

Siegel, D. J. (2015). *Brainstorm: The power and purpose of the teenage brain.* TarcherPerigee.

Siegel, D. J. (2020a). *Aware: The science and practice of presence.* TarcherPerigee.

Siegel, D. J. (2020b). *The Developing Mind: How relationships and the brain interact to shape who we are.* The Guilford Press.

Siegel, D. J. (2022). *IntraConnected: MWe (Me + We) as the integration of self, identity, and belonging* (Audiobook). Brilliance Audio.

Siegel, D. J., & Bryson, T. P. (2012). *The whole-brain child: 12 revolutionary strategies to nurture your child's developing mind.* Random House.

Siegel, D. J., & Bryson, T. P. (2014). *No-drama discipline: The whole-brain way to calm the chaos and nurture your child's developing mind.* Bantam Books.

Siegel, D. J., & Bryson, T. P. (2019). *The yes brain: How to cultivate courage, curiosity, and resilience in your child.* Bantam Books.

Siegel, D. J., & Bryson, T. P. (2021). *The power of showing up: How parental presence shapes who our kids become and how their brains get wired.* Ballantine Books.

Siegel, D. J., & Rutsch, E. (2012). *Dialogs on how to build a culture of empathy.* [Video]. YouTube. https://youtu.be/XIzTdXdhU0w?feature=shared

Siegel, D. J., & Hartzell, M. (2013). *Parenting from the inside out: How a deeper self-understanding can help you raise children who thrive.* TarcherPerigee.

Sinek, S. (2011). *Start with why: How great leaders inspire everyone to take action.* Portfolio.

Stone, C. (2019). *Holy noticing: The Bible, your brain, and the mindful space between moments.* Moody Publishers.

Taylor, J. B. TEDX. (2008, March 13). *Jill Bolte Taylor. My stroke of insight* [Video]. YouTube. https://www.youtube.com/watch?v=UyyjU8fzEYU

TerKeurst, L. (2018). *It's not supposed to be this way: Finding unexpected strength when disappointments leave you shattered.* Thomas Nelson.

TerKeurst, L. (2019, November 29). *Can I really trust God?* [Blog]. Encouragement for Today. https://lysaterkeurst.com/2019/11/12/can-i-really-trust-god/

TerKeurst, L. (2023). *Forgiving what you can't forget: A practical guide on how to heal, forgive the past and move on, make peace with painful relationships and overcome your emotional wounds.* Independently published.

Treleaven, D. A. (2018). *Trauma-sensitive mindfulness: Practices for safe and transformative healing.* W. W. Norton & Company.

van der Kolk, B. (2015). *The body keeps the score: Brain, mind, and body in the healing of trauma.* Penguin Books.

van der Kolk, B. (2019). *A quickstart guide: How to work with the traumatized brain* [Course]. National Institute for the Clinical Application of Behavioral Medicine. https://www.nicabm.com/program/trauma-vdk/

Vine, W. E. (1996). *Vine's Complete Expository Dictionary of Old and New Testament Words.* Nelson.

Warner, M., & Coursey, C. M. (2023). *The 4 habits of joy-filled people: 15 minute brain science hacks to a more connected and satisfying life.* Northfield Publishing.

Warner, M., & Wilder, J. (2016). *Rare leadership: 4 uncommon habits for increasing trust, joy, and engagement in the people you lead.* Moody Publishers.

Wilder, E. J., Khouri, E. M., Coursey, C. M., & Sutton, S. D. (2013). *Joy starts here: The transformation zone.* Independently published.

Wilder, J. (2020). *Renovated: God, Dallas Willard, and the church that transforms.* NavPress.

Wilder, J., & Woolridge, R. (2022). *Escaping enemy mode: How our brains unite or divide us.* Moody Publishers.

Willard, D. (2019). *Life without lack: Living in the fullness of Psalm 23.* Zondervan.

Willard, D. (2021). *Hearing God: Developing a conversational relationship with God.* IVP Formatio.

Williams, C. (Ed.). (2008). *Who would you be without your story? Dialogues with Byron Katie.* Hay House Inc.

Williams, P., & Menendez, D. S. (2015). *Becoming a professional life coach: Lessons from the Institute of Life Coach Training* (2nd Ed.). W. W. Norton & Company.

# RECOMMENDED READING AND RESOURCES

"7 Habits of Highly Effective People," by Stephen Covey

"Anatomy of the Soul," by Curt Thompson, M.D.

"Anchored," by Deb Dana

"Anxiety at Work," by Adrian Gostick and Chester Elton

"Atlas of the Heart," by Brene Brown

"Atomic Habits," by James Clear

"Aware," by Daniel J. Siegel, M.D.

"Be Your Future Self Now," by Dr. Benjamin Hardy

"Becoming a Professional Life Coach," by Patrick Williams and Diane Menendez

"Becoming Supernatural," by Joe Dispenza

"Better Decisions, Fewer Regrets," by Andy Stanley

"Boundaries," by Henry Cloud and John Townsend

"Boundary Boss," by Terri Cole

"Brainstorm," by Daniel J. Siegel, M.D.

"Braving the Wilderness," by Brene Brown

"Breath," by James Nestor

"Call of the Wild," by Kimberly Ann Johnson

"Care of Souls," by David G. Brenner

"Change Your Questions, Change Your Life," by Marilee Adams, Ph.D.

"Christian Coaching," by Gary Collins

"Coaching with the Brain in Mind," by David Rock and Linda J. Page, Ph.D.

"Crafting a Rule of Life," by Stephen A. Macchia

"Crucial Conversations," by Joseph Grenny, Kerry Patterson, et al.

"Dangerous Prayers," by Craig Groeschel

# Transform Your Brain

"Daring Greatly," by Brene Brown

"Dream Big," by Bob Goff

"Embracing Radical Responsibility," by Fleet Maull, Ph.D.

"Emotional Agility," by Susan David

"Emotional Intelligence," by Daniel Goleman

"Escaping Enemy Mode," by Jim Wilder, Ray Woolridge, et al.

"Fierce Conversations," by Susan Scott

"Fierce Leadership," by Susan Scott

"Fierce Self-Compassion," by Dr. Kristin Neff

"Forgiving What You Can't Forget," by Lysa TerKeurst

"Healing Trauma," by Peter A. Levine, Ph.D.

"Hearing God," by Dallas Willard

"Helping People Change," by Richard Boyatzis, et al.

"Holy Noticing," by Charles Stone

"How Emotions Are Made," by Lisa Feldman Barrett

"How to Be Loving," by Danielle LaPorte

"How to Win Friends & Influence People," by Dale Carnegie

"IntraConnected," by Daniel J. Siegel, M.D.

"Invitation to Solitude and Silence," by Ruth Haley Barton

"It's Not Always Depression," by Hilary Jacobs Hendel

"It's Not Supposed to Be This Way," by Lysa TerKeurst

"Joy Starts Here," by Dr. E. James Wilder, et al.

"Leading Well From Within," by Daniel Friedland, M.D.

"Life Without Lack," by Dallas Willard

"Mansions of the Heart," by R. Thomas Ashbrook

"Marching Off the Map," by Tim Elmore

"Mindfulness and the Brain," by Jack Kornfield, Ph.D., and Daniel J. Siegel, M.D.

"Mindset," by Carol S. Dweck, Ph.D.

"Mindsight," by Daniel J. Siegel, M.D.

"Moving Beyond Trauma," by Ilene Smith

"No Bad Parts," by Dr. Richard C. Schwartz, Ph.D.

"No-Drama Discipline," by Daniel J. Siegel, M.D., and Tina Payne Bryson, Ph.D.

"Nonviolent Communication," by Marshall Rosenberg

"Parenting from the Inside Out," by Daniel J. Siegel, M.D., and Mary Hartzell, M.Ed.

"Polyvagal Practices," by Deb Dana

"Positive Intelligence," by Shirzad Chamine

"Present over Perfect," by Shauna Niequist

"Quiet Leadership," by David Rock

"Rare Leadership," by Marcus Warner and Jim Wilder

"Renovated," by Jim Wilder

"Resilient," by John Eldredge

"Rising Strong," by Brene Brown

"Set Boundaries, Find Peace," by Nedra Glover Tawwab

"Social Intelligence," by Daniel Goleman, Ph.D.

"Start with Why," by Simon Sinek

"Switch On Your Brain," by Dr. Caroline Leaf

"The 4 habits of Joy-Filled Peole, by Marcus Warner and Chris Coursey

"The 15 Commitments of Conscious Leadership," by Jim Dethmer, Diana Chapman, et al.

"The 15 Irrefutable Laws of Growth," by John C. Maxwell

"The 21 Irrefutable Laws of Leadership," by John C. Maxwell

"The Attentive Life," by Leighton Ford

# Transform Your Brain

"The Body Keeps the Score," by Bessel van der Kolk, M.D.

"The Body Remembers," by Babette Rothschild

"The Burnout Challenge," by Christina Maslach and Michael P. Leiter

"The Developing Mind," by Daniel J. Siegel, M.D.

"The Eight Paradoxes of Great Leadership," by Tim Elmore

"The Enneagram," by Richard Rohr and Andreas Ebert

"The Fearless Organization," by Amy C. Edmondson

"The Five Dysfunctions of a Team," by Patrick Lencioni

"The Gift of Presence," by Caroline Welch

"The Gifts of Imperfection," by Brene Brown

"The Healing Power of Emotion," edited by Diana Fosha, Daniel J. Siegel, and Marion F. Solomon

"The Joy Switch," by Chris M. Coursey

"The Leadership Pause," by Chris L. Johnson, Ph.D.

"The Mindful Self-Compassion Workbook," by Kristin Neff, Ph.D., and Christopher Germer, Ph.D.

"The Myth of Normal," by Gabor Maté

"The Pocket Guide to Polyvagal Theory," by Stephen W. Porges

"The Power of Habit," by Charles Duhigg

"The Power of Positive Thinking," by Norman Vincent Peale

"The Power of Showing Up," by Daniel J. Siegel, M.D., and Tina Payne Bryson, Ph.D.

"The Power of Vulnerability," by Brene Brown

"The Road Back to You," by Ian Morgan Cron and Suzanne Stabile

"The Soul of Shame," by Curt Thompson, M.D.

"The Stress Prescription," by Elissa Epel, Ph.D.

"The Teenage Brain," by Frances E. Jensen and Amy Ellis Nutt

"The Whole-Brain Child," by Daniel J. Siegel, M.D., and Tina Payne Bryson, Ph.D.

"The Yes Brain," by Daniel J. Siegel, M.D., and Tina Payne Bryson, Ph.D.

"Think Again," by Adam Grant

"Thinking, Fast and Slow," by Daniel Kahneman

"Trauma and Memory," by Peter A. Levine, Ph.D.

"Trauma-Sensitive Mindfulness," by David A. Treleaven

"Understanding the Ennegram," by Don Richard Riso and Russ Hudson

"Unhackable," by Kary Oberbrunner

"Visioneering," by Andy Stanley

"Waking the Tiger," by Peter Levine

"Who Would You Be Without Your Story? Dialogues with Byron Katie," edited by Carol Williams

"Whole Brain Living," by Jill Bolte Taylor, Ph.D.

"Your Body Is Your Brain," by Amanda Blake

"Your Brain at Work," by Dr. David Rock

# ACKNOWLEDGMENTS

Thank you for investing your time in the journey toward wholeness, which continues to unfold as we abandon survival living and live an integrated life of abundance.

This book is a journey of my healing by applying the work of scientists, authors, researchers, and frontrunners in interpersonal neurobiology, positive intelligence, somatic coaching, polyvagal theory, trauma experts, and conscious leadership, as well as thought leaders in neurotheology. I am deeply grateful for those who have influenced many of the thoughts you see written in this book. For those whose work I have cited in this book and who contribute to the advancement of many, the world is indebted — Daniel Siegel, Amanda Blake, Daniel Goleman, Kristin Neff, Carol Dweck, David Rock, Christina Maslach, Daniel Friedland, Lisa Feldman Barrett, David Treleaven, Richard Boyatzis, Ann Betz, Jim Dethmer, Staci Haines, Deb Dana, Stephen Porges, Gabor Maté, Elissa Epel, Shirzad Chamine, Jim Wilder, Dallas Willard, Marcus Warner, Chris Coursey, Allan Schore, Charles Stone, Curt Thompson,

Daniel Kahneman, Hilary Jacobs Hendel, Bessel van der Kolk, Daniel Amen, Jill Bolte Taylor, Fleet Maull, Brene Brown, Rick Hansen, Babette Rothschild, Terri Cole, Nedra Glover Tawwab, Peter Levine, Richard Schwartz, Pat Ogden, Benjamin Hardy, Kimberly Ann Johnson, Arielle Schwartz, and many others. Thank you for your decades of research, passion, and influence for change in this world.

My thanks to the community and leaders at the Kingdom Builders Academy. Thank you Tamara Lowe, for creating the path to publishing, Rae Lynne Johnson, Tom Griffith and all the coaches for holding my hand through writing and publishing this book. Your step-by-step guidance was invaluable! It would not have happened without you. Thank you to the Christian Writer Group at CCNI-Christian Coaches Network International for your valuable input on the second edition. Thank you, Edie Edmondson, for your miraculous and patient editing of the first edition. Your attention to detail and precision is beyond any other! Thank you for improving on my work and making it more digestible to the reader. Thank you, Andie Plunkett, for your amazing work on the graphics and most of all your friendship.

Multiple coaching certifications from and the influence of these masterful coaches have fueled my journey of growth. I'd like to thank Cheryl Scanlan, Christopher McCluskey, Kim Avery, Andrew Gorter, Jordan Mercedes, Michael Marx, and Pamela Mertz for your investment in my growth and development as an International Coaching Federation-certified coach and Christian Coaches Network International-certified coach. Also, a big shout out goes to Jon Berhoff, Adair Cates, Stephen Bouchard, and all the brilliant minds from the xchange approach community for building in skills that will last a lifetime. As an xchange approach certified guide, the way I do business has been transformed. My heart is overflowing with gratitude and love for you all.

To my dear friend, daily business building accountability partner, and colleague, Vicki Terrill — we are in this together, and I would not want to build a business without you. Your brilliant strategic thinking has kept this "pantser" dreaming big and walking in my vision. Thank you for listening through the tears, frustration, and joys of building a coaching business from the ground floor up. Oh, what a journey it has been! "You complete me" ("Jerry Maguire"), and I cannot wait to see what God continues to do through us!

Thank you, Richard, Anna, Ben, Sarah, my sister Kim, my family, and all my supportive friends (you know who you are) for your constant support as I continue to build a business from scratch and follow my dream of moving others toward wholeness. Yes, you know the many failures that accompanied the successes on this journey, and you never stopped believing in me. I'm eternally grateful for your love and encouragement.

To the One and Only God, who gave me the words, planted the dream in my heart, and gave me the power through His Spirit to accomplish the calling. When I was weak, He was strong in and through me.

Soli Deo Gloria.

www.ingramcontent.com/pod-product-compliance
Lightning Source LLC
LaVergne TN
LVHW061608070526
838199LV00078B/7208